811.008 W615c

Visiting Walt

## DATE DUE

| | | |
|---|---|---|
| | | |
| | | |
| | | |
| | | |
| | | |
| | | |
| | | |
| | | |
| | | |
| | | |
| | | |
| | | |
| | | |
| | | |
| | | |
| | | |

DEMCO 38-297

2004

# Visiting Walt

# THE IOWA WHITMAN SERIES

Ed Folsom, *series editor*

# Visiting
# Walt

Poems Inspired

by the Life & Work of

WALT WHITMAN

edited by

SHEILA COGHILL &

THOM TAMMARO

Foreword by Ed Folsom

UNIVERSITY OF

IOWA PRESS ψ Iowa City

University of Iowa Press, Iowa City 52242

Copyright © 2003 by the University of Iowa Press

All rights reserved

Printed in the United States of America

Design by Richard Hendel

http://www.uiowa.edu/uiowapress

The publication of this book was generously supported
by the University of Iowa Foundation.

Printed on acid-free paper

Library of Congress Cataloging-in-Publication Data
Visiting Walt: poems inspired by the life and work of Walt
Whitman / edited by Sheila Coghill and Thom Tammaro; foreword
by Ed Folsom.
p.     cm.—(The Iowa Whitman series)
Includes index.
ISBN 0-87745-853-7 (cloth), ISBN 0-87745-854-5 (pbk.)
1. Whitman, Walt, 1819–1892—Poetry.   2. American poetry.
3. Poets—Poetry.   I. Coghill, Sheila, 1952–.   II. Tammaro,
Thom.   III. Series.
PS595.W42V575 2003
811.008′0351—dc21              2002043047

03  04  05  06  07  C  5  4  3  2  1
03  04  05  06  07  P  5  4  3  2  1

Poets to come! orators, singers, musicians to come!

Not to-day is to justify me and answer what I am for,

But you, a new brood, native, athletic, continental, greater than

before known,

Arouse! for you must justify me.

—Walt Whitman, "Poets to Come"

# Contents

# Foreword

ED FOLSOM

One of my most exhilarating reading experiences last year was *Visiting Emily*, Sheila Coghill and Thom Tammaro's revelatory collection of poetic responses to Emily Dickinson. I had been aware of a number of poems about Dickinson, but I was astonished to discover the range and variety represented in *Visiting Emily*. I did, however, know something about poets' responses to Walt Whitman, since, along with Jim Perlman and Dan Campion, I had edited *Walt Whitman: The Measure of His Song* (1981; 1998), which gathered essays and poems from Whitman's time to the present, documenting the long history of poets talking back to Whitman. So, when Coghill and Tammaro proposed to edit a companion volume to their Dickinson book, one focusing on Whitman, my first thought was that there was no need for such a project. But the more I found out about their intentions, the more convinced I became that *Visiting Walt* would be the unique and illuminating collection it has in fact turned out to be. This is a book about Whitman that contains *only* poems, and only one poem per poet. Although there is certainly a historical breadth in *Visiting Walt*, the book is not a chronological record of the long conversation poets have had with Whitman since the late nineteenth century but rather a kind of explosion of poetic encounters, a hundred distinct sites of creative interaction with Whitman, each igniting into a poem.

Reading these hundred poems is like looking at a clear night sky: it's a vast spectrum of varying points of light, coming from different distances and different times, and all, impossibly, drawn through some massive gravitational pull toward Walt Whitman. *Visiting Walt* powerfully presents this array of poems and then quietly sits back and invites the reader to begin tracing constellations, patterns, interrelationships. This is a book built on Whitman's belief, as he described it in *Democratic Vistas*, "that the process of reading is not a half-sleep, but, in highest sense, an exercise, a gymnast's struggle; that the reader is to do something for himself, must be on the alert, must himself or herself construct indeed the poem, argument, history, metaphysical essay — the text furnishing the hints, the clue, the start or frame-work."

Whitman would have been pleased with the big round number — a hundred poems by a hundred poets — that Coghill and Tammaro offer in *Visiting Walt*. He was always fascinated with numbers, and in 1857, as he was planning the largest expansion of *Leaves of Grass* that he would ever undertake, he wrote, "I have now *a hundred* poems ready." He liked the full feel of that number, which, he believed, would give the book "an aspect of completeness": "I shall have, as I said, a hundred poems . . . *that* must be the true Leaves of Grass." It would have made Whitman happy to hear this robust group of a hundred poets talking back to him, arguing with him, celebrating him, questioning him, debating him, joking with him. These hundred "poets to come" in fact round off Whitman's work and give it "an aspect of completeness" by answering the challenge he issued nearly a hundred and fifty years ago:

Poets to come! . . .
Not to-day is to justify me and answer what I am for,
But you, a new brood, native, athletic, continental, greater than before known,
Arouse! for you must justify me.

I myself but write one or two indicative words for the future,

.  .  .  .  .  .  .  .  .  .  .  .  .  .  .  .  .  .  .  .  .  .  .

Leaving it to you to prove and define it,
Expecting the main things from you.

In making this call, Whitman was inventing the original "reader-response" poetry, work that demands that the reader join the poet in the act of creation: "Not the book needs so much to be the complete thing, but the reader of the book does," he said. What makes the poets in *Visiting Walt* so remarkable is that, in these poems, they are at once perceptive readers *and* active writers, offering insights into Whitman's work while creating new work that both builds upon and deviates from his. By limiting each poet to one poem and by presenting the poets alphabetically, Sheila Coghill and Thom Tammaro present a democratic catalog of the vast response to Whitman. Here are many voices, varied and equal — male, female, black, white, American Indian, North American, South American, English, Spanish, gay, straight, alive, dead. Here are a hundred poems that *read* Whitman's poems in a hundred different ways, that remake Whitman again and again, that answer what he is for.

# Expecting the Main Things

Early on in our gathering of poems for the manuscript that eventually became the anthology *Visiting Emily: Poems Inspired by the Life and Work of Emily Dickinson*, we both realized that the questions we were asking about Emily Dickinson were, for the most part, questions we could ask of Whitman: among hundreds of American poets, why does he, like Dickinson, evoke such varied response? Like Dickinson (and Robert Frost), why does Whitman's popularity among general readers supersede that of other poets? Who, at some time in his or her education, has not encountered the sweeping assertions "I celebrate myself, and sing myself, / And what I assume you shall assume" of "Song of Myself," or the elegiac, melancholy beauty of "When Lilacs Last in the Dooryard Bloom'd"? How many schoolchildren committed to memory "O Captain! My Captain!"? Why is it that anyone serious about the art and craft of poetry, must—at some point in his or her life—confront, in love or in scorn, the monolithic presence of Walt Whitman?

But while Emily Dickinson's poetry creates among her followers feelings of charm, protectiveness, and awe, Whitman seems to ignite his followers. In "A Pact" Ezra Pound sharply captures the love-hate relationship many American writers have with Walt Whitman's poetry when he asserts "I have detested you long enough. / I come to you as a grown child / Who has had a pig-headed father; / . . . We have one sap and one root— / Let there be commerce between us." This resolve, this going back to Whitman as the "father" of American poetry, is readily seen in the many tributes included in this anthology. Whitman indeed has many children. There are as many Walt Whitmans as there are writers who have been inspired by his life and work, creating successive generations of poetry "out of the cradle [and] endlessly rocking." This is a process he himself encouraged (well, at least he did not discourage it!).

1855. *Leaves of Grass*. Has there ever been a year or a book—before or after—so important, so vital, to the life of American poetry? And Walt Whitman. Has there ever been a poet—before or after—so central to the life of American poetry? Consider him sensational, mystical, erotic, and expansive; consider him the good gray poet, the moral crusader, the prophet of Democracy, and the enemy of social injustice; or consider him libertarian, lecherous, homosexual, perverted, unsavory, inconsistent, passionate, macho, masculine, feminine, androgynous, rebellious, ideological, controversial, or subversive (of course, he is all of these and he was aware of these assessments in his own time)—there is no getting around his genius for liberating poetry from the stultifying "emotional slither" (Pound's indictment of Victorian poetry) of the nineteenth century. Whitman is the architect of American vers libre. As Annie Finch has written in her intriguing study *The Ghost of Meter: Culture and Prosody in American Free Verse*, "For American poets in general, Longfellow's hexameters [in *Evangeline*] and Whitman's triple rhythms were crucial in establishing a new freedom of resources, an enlarged metrical vocabulary. Remarkably quickly the 'new' metrical mode came to carry a connotative weight capable of balancing the four centuries of iambic pentameter's hegemony." Whitman holds the door open for generations of writers to pass through as they "simmer" their way toward true poetry. This anthology, we hope, represents a diverse group of writers who have come to terms with their "pig-headed father."

Perhaps Walt Whitman remains imprinted in our minds because he *is* everywhere. He was never camera shy: we have over 130 photographic images of him, from the swaggering, youthful portraits of the 1840s to the pensive, meditative good gray poet images of the late 1880s and early 1890s. And perhaps he haunts us because he is likely the first recorded American poet. On an 1890 wax cylinder recording, a voice thought to be Whitman's reads his six-line poem "America" (asserting as always that America is the "Centre of equal daughters, equal sons").

Whitman is the democratic poet par excellence and is everywhere accessible in his democratic immanence. Jorge Luis Borges recalls, "The smell of coffee and of newspapers / . . . lazily he fills / The weary mirror with his gaze. His eyes / See a face. Unsurprised he thinks: That face / Is me. . . . / His voice declares: / I'm almost gone and yet my verses scan / Life and its splendor. I was Walt Whitman." And Pablo Neruda reconstructs a liberating first encounter with the poet: "I don't remember / at what age / or where, / whether in the great wet South / or on the terrifying / coast, . . . / I touched a hand and it was / the hand of Walt Whitman." Erica Jong captures Whitman's ecstasy of being: "Unhappiness is cheap . . . / I say to hell with the analysts of minus & plus, / the life-shrinkers, the diminishers of joy. / I say to hell with anyone / who would suck on misery / like a pacifier / in a toothless mouth. / I say to hell with gloom."

Never deliberately inscrutable, Whitman equally inspires imagining in a variety of contexts from the irreverent to the sublime. Thomas Lux memorializes Whitman's dying wish as a bungled autopsy: "At his request, after death, his brain was removed / for science, phrenology, to study, and / as the mortuary assistant carried it (I suppose / in a jar but I hope cupped / in his hands) across the lab's stone floor, he dropped it. . . . dropped and shattered, a cosmos, / on the floor. . . ." Federico García Lorca lovingly resurrects Whitman from a "New York of mud, . . . of wire and death" in his "Ode to Walt Whitman," chanting "Not a single moment, old beautiful Walt Whitman, / have I stopped seeing your beard full of butterflies," and sees him as an "old man beautiful as the cloud / who cried like a bird / with his sex pierced by a needle, / enemy of the satyr, / enemy of the vine / and lover of bodies under the heavy cloth." And our contemporary, Sherman Alexie, envisions Whitman watching young Indian boys playing basketball: "stretches his calf muscles / . . . His huge beard is ridiculous on the reservation / . . . He wants to run. He hardly has the patience to wait for his turn. / 'What's the score?' he asks. . . . / Basketball is like this for Walt Whitman. He watches these Indian boys / as if they were the last bodies on earth. Every body is brown! / Walt Whitman shakes because he believes in God. / Walt Whitman dreams of the Indian boy who will defend him."

Wildness multiplies in imagining Walt Whitman, for all that we can know about him and his poetry is what we can know about ourselves. Aliki Barnstone's "Wild With It," for example: "I am your underground river, flowing in the dark / beneath the earth's skin, and I am your blood. / . . . I am a Greek island redolent with oregano and thyme, / dry salt air. I am the sea voluptuous against your naked thighs, / the sunlight drying the blond hairs on your legs and arms. / . . . I am your world wide web, I am your easy chair— / . . . I am I am I am. And in you I am, for you erase / and make new our two conjugating shapes." Whitman is unruly, impertinent; he flaunts yet embraces all moods. If, as Howard Nemerov states in "A Modern Poet," Whitman "given a Ford / Foundation Fellowship, he'd buy a Ford," Sharon Olds's "Nurse Whitman" sees him "move between the soldiers' cots / the way I move among my dead / their white bodies laid out in lines. / . . . You write their letters home. I take the dictation / . . . They die and you still feel them."

Ever catalyzing, whimsically or calculatingly unapologetic, we cannot know, except to know that Whitman deliberately taunts us with the confidence of knowing so much about the world, the body, the self, the nation, the cosmos. Inevitably then, Whitman's vastness makes itself known and felt in our poetry as the all-encompassing corrective to the Puritan via negativa transplanted in the American psyche. Transfiguring the shadows of democracy by saying them into being, Whitman invites America to examine its own boot soles, articulates a democracy so radical it leaves no room for sentimental patriotism, embraces every marginalized individual so thoroughly and in such a militant poetic voice writ large by shocking imagery that we often lose sight of the fact that his method was often a cultivated, hyperbolic posturing. He believed, as Whitman critic and biographer David Reynolds states in *Beneath the American Renaissance*, that "social corruptions . . . could be overcome only by passionate defiance. 'Give us turbulence, give us excitement' [Whitman] wrote." And Whitman *gives* writers this excitement, this permission to *go wild*, to "turn and live with the animals."

Ever endearing, dear Walt salutes us while we salute him! Lynn Emanuel expresses this impulse that many writers have, this mirroring need to acknowledge Whitman in their own reflections: "from the back streets of Pittsburgh / from the little lit window in the attic / of my mind where I sit brooding and smoking / like a hot iron, Walt, I salute you! / Here we are. In Love! In a Poem! / . . . My every dark and slanderous thought. Walt I salute you!" Whitman is dear to us because he *is* us and he lets us be ourselves. Anyone who aspires to write can at least pretend to be Walt Whitman as a starting point—without embarrassment and without self-consciousness! Strangely, or logically, we are all "one sap and one root" when we enter Whitman's world.

Because of the nature of his public persona and the undeniable presence of his work during his own lifetime, he was, in his own time, the subject of well-deserved homage, while others found him the easy target of parody. And it has continued ever since. Ed Folsom has written brilliantly about this in his documentary essays "Talking Back to Walt Whitman: An Introduction" and "The Poets Respond: A Bibliographic Chronology," both in *Walt Whitman: The Measure of His Song* (Holy Cow! Press, 1981; 1998), a necessary anthology for anyone's Whitman collection or poetry bookshelf. In these essays, Folsom clearly demonstrates the extent of this phenomenon, occurring as early as the 1860s from both American and British writers, with the parodies themselves collected in the 1923 anthology *Parodies on Walt Whitman*. Likewise, special issues of magazines and journals have paid homage over the years, such as the *Beloit Poetry Journal* in 1954 and *American Dialog* in 1969. The journals *West Hills Review* and *Mickle Street Review* have devoted space in their many issues for poems about Whitman. In *Visiting Walt*, then, we are pleased to present poems that have appeared over the years in some of these journals and books. Of course, there are hundreds of more poems inspired by the life and work of Walt Whitman that are not included here. We hope our "Whitman sampler" of 100 poems by 100 poets is at once a companion anthology to *Visiting Emily* and a reminder and renewal as we cross over to the new millennium — now a third century of poems and poets inspired by the life and work of Walt Whitman — of the centrality of Walt Whitman's influence on American and global literature.

No matter how far we stray, Walt Whitman is always with us, sauntering along. Our eyes have met his casual glance, we feel his presence in the writing room, at the writing desk, peering lovingly over our shoulders, nudging us along. We think the poems included here bear Whitman's inheritance — both in their allusions to Whitman's life and work and in their depths of undeniable resonance with Whitman's spirit. We think he would be happy — but never satisfied — with their justifications. We think he would be happy with them, but we also know he would be looking ahead to the next poem, the next generation, ready to move on, waiting for us somewhere. In all of the poems we can hear Whitman "whispering . . . whispering." We hope his expectations have been met.

As editors, we take full responsibility for any errors in the collection. We will make every effort to correct any errors we discover — or those brought to our attention by readers — should the collection go into a second printing or edition. As with all such projects, there are many people to thank. We would like to begin by thanking the many writers here for their generosity, support, enthusiasm, and patience with us during the editing process. We also would like to thank the many editors and publishers who helped arrange permissions to reprint the poems. Once again, we are grateful to Holly Carver, director of the University of Iowa Press, and her staff for their enthusiasm, professionalism, and support throughout the project. We also owe an immeasurable debt to Ed Folsom who, early on, met with us and provided good counsel, then took time from his busy life to write his foreword. Anyone who has met Ed knows that his generosity and spirit are truly Whitmanesque!

We would also like to thank our many friends and colleagues at Minnesota State University Moorhead for their support and assistance. A special thanks goes to Shelly Heng, Dee Kruger, David Leukam, Kristin Stenlund, and Andrew Torpen for assisting us with typing and preparing the manuscript. We would be remiss if we did not thank the professional librarians at Livingston Lord Library at Minnesota State University Moorhead for their assistance. We are especially grateful to Electronic Resources Librarian Stacey Voeller, former student and now colleague, and to Dianne Schmidt, library technician in the Interlibrary Loan Department, who helped us track down numerous poems and rare and out-of-print books in a timely manner. Finally, we would like to thank the Minnesota State University Moorhead Alumni Foundation Office for its continuing support.

# Visiting Walt

# Defending Walt Whitman

Basketball is like this for young Indian boys, all arms and legs
and serious stomach muscles. Every body is brown!
These are the twentieth-century warriors who will never kill,
although a few sat quietly in the deserts of Kuwait,
waiting for orders to do something, do something.

God, there is nothing as beautiful as a jump shot
on a reservation summer basketball court
where the ball is moist with sweat
and makes a sound when it swishes through the net
that causes Walt Whitman to weep because it is so perfect.

There are veterans of foreign wars here,
whose bodies are still dominated
by collarbones and knees, whose bodies still respond
in the ways that bodies are supposed to respond when we are young.
Every body is brown! Look there, that boy can run
up and down this court forever. He can leap for a rebound
with his back arched like a salmon, all meat and bone
synchronized, magnetic, as if the court were a river,
as if the rim were a dam, as if the air were a ladder
leading the Indian boy toward home.

Some of the Indian boys still wear their military haircuts
while a few have let their hair grow back.
It will never be the same as it was before!
One Indian boy has never cut his hair, not once, and he braids it
into wild patterns that do not measure anything.
He is just a boy with too much time on his hands.
Look at him. He wants to play this game in bare feet.

God, the sun is so bright! There is no place like this.
Walt Whitman stretches his calf muscles
on the sidelines. He has the next game.
His huge beard is ridiculous on the reservation.
Some body throws a crazy pass and Walt Whitman catches it with quick hands.
He brings the ball close to his nose
and breathes in all of its smells: leather, brown skin, sweat, black hair,
burning oil, twisted ankle, long drink of warm water,
gunpowder, pine tree. Walt Whitman squeezes the ball tightly.
He wants to run. He hardly has the patience to wait for his turn.
"What's the score?" he asks. He asks, "What's the score?"

Basketball is like this for Walt Whitman. He watches these Indian boys
as if they were the last bodies on earth. Every body is brown!
Walt Whitman shakes because he believes in God.
Walt Whitman dreams of the Indian boy who will defend him,
trapping him in the corner, all flailing arms and legs
and legendary stomach muscles. Walt Whitman shakes
because he believes in God. Walt Whitman dreams
of the first jump shot he will take, the ball arcing clumsily
from his fingers, striking the rim so hard that it sparks.
Walt Whitman shakes because he believes in God.
Walt Whitman closes his eyes. He is a small man and his beard
is ludicrous on the reservation, absolutely insane.
His beard makes the Indian boys laugh righteously. His beard frightens
the smallest Indian boys. His beard tickles the skin
of the Indian boys who dribble past him. His beard, his beard!

God, there is beauty in every body. Walt Whitman stands
at center court while the Indian boys run from basket to basket.
Walt Whitman cannot tell the difference between
offense and defense. He does not care if he touches the ball.
Half of the Indian boys wear T-shirts damp with sweat
and the other half are bareback, skin slick and shiny.
There is no place like this. Walt Whitman smiles.
Walt Whitman shakes. This game belongs to him.

# Walt Whitman and the Birds

*Translated by Alexis Levitin*

On waking up, I remembered Peter Doyle. It must have been
six o'clock, and in the Mimosa tree across the way a bird was
singing. I won't swear it was singing in English, only
Virginia Woolf's birds have such privileges, but the jubilation
of my bullfinch led me to remember the skylark of American
meadows and the chilled face of the young Irishman whom
Walt Whitman loved that winter, seated at the back of the
tavern, rubbing his hands, close to the heat of the stove.

I opened the window and, in the first thin light that was
approaching, searched in vain for the spotless joy that had
awakened me. But suddenly, one, two, three moist trills
sounded, leading me to a puff of feathers one could scarcely
tell from the leaves. Then, invoking ancient metaphors of
song, I turned to the venerated book in my hand and, stanza
by stanza, opened the flood-gates to the waters of being, like
one who prepares himself for flight.

# Wild With It

*You will hardly know who I am or what I mean,*
*But I shall be good health to you nevertheless,*
*And filter and fibre your blood.*
— Walt Whitman

I am your underground river, flowing in the dark
beneath the earth's skin, and I am your blood.

I am the Mississippi, lighted and calm,
and the grassy hills clambering from its waters,

and I am your Mississippi flooding its banks, a volcano
flaming the sky to ash, a tidal wave. Because of you,

I am a Greek island redolent with oregano and thyme,
dry salt air. I am the sea voluptuous against your naked thighs,

the sunlight drying the blond hairs on your legs and arms.
I am your sun burning away all sight except its own light,

a sun throbbing, giving the land color and shape,
the little whitewashed house, the bed below the window full

of mountains breathing deep into the earth, bones of knees,
elbows, flesh of breasts and cocks, cunts and shoulders,

broad chest where the heart beats and makes the capers
and daisies tremble, all the nerves, thistles and sticks,

electric and telephone wires buzzing on your flesh.
I am the moonlight showing you how the sea's body stretches

all the way to New York, to streets whitened by oil and rain,
to shoes scuffing the sidewalks, and windows bright

with pots and pans dangling from the ceiling,
lovers and families, bathrooms — a guy's bent head

as he fills the bowl — I am pens, notebooks, computer screens,
I am your world wide web, I am your easy chair —

you hold a book on your knee — mine is the bare belly
appearing before the shade goes down and mine is

the kiss deepening to a bite on your neck.
I am your witch poking pins into a voodoo doll.

She who comes between us I will burn, bury, break,
shoot off in a rocket to the nothing of space.

*I am I am I am.* And in you I am, for you erase
and make new our two conjugating shapes.

# Hair of the Field

*Bitter (Anglo-Saxon biter). Original meaning, "biting, cutting,*
*sharp," but now used only of taste. Also, unpalatable*
*to the mind. Expressing or betokening intense grief, misery,*
*or affliction of spirit.*

Our front yard bursts with clover and dandelions
and long spears of rye and pampas grass

where frizzled neighborhood cats
stalk beetles and roll on their backs.

We are the shame of our neat buzz-cut street,
but we have no lawnmower,

so today my task is to crop this savannah
with a pair of garden shears.

I give the yard a trim and think of Walt Whitman
growing hair underground, his fingers worming

through the soil, green nails clawing toward light.
Passersby stop and smile at me, ridiculous

with my pathetic clippers, but I adjust my baseball cap,
and I am Walt Whitman, young, strong in a teeshirt,

covered in pollen and sweat,
all rude muscle working through the grass.

At the graveyard up the block the beautiful hair
is shaved close to the graves.

It's nice to think the dead push up
into the world as ragweed and sorrel,

the way Walt's words become grass in the mouth,
his delicious syllables: *the smallest sprout shows*

*there is really no death*. Truth is, the smallest sprout
shows its silver underbelly as I slice off its legs.

As I murder grass, it exhales last puffs
of pollen I cough up like bitter seeds.

I am clipping Whitman's nails and thinking about
the tangle underneath out of which rises

even a simple word, like *bitter*,
thinking what would it be like to follow a word back

into the mouth and swim down the column of air
through the babble of centuries?

I open my eyes in a dank Saxon cottage.
There is the smell of cabbage and whale oil.

I have just bitten into a sour apple,
a taste that bites the mouth, and as I spit

the apple flesh onto the floor I cough out
a new word, *biter*. Bitter, bitter.

It rises from the stomach, and it tastes like acid
and loss. It tastes like grass.

Within a year I use the word to name
the taste of a broken longboat, my girl's red hair

sinking in the frozen lake, my land
overrun by people speaking another tongue.

I am standing in a field. And I dive down
the length of a blade of grass underground.

Here all things take shape, rooted in each other,
so the moon that spilled honey on Whitman's head

will be overhead tonight, and long after
the longboat has become a skeleton

half in sand, and the child a seed
in the lakebottom's mud, I taste the biting taste

of grapefruit, appleseed, and go back
into the house with my hands stained green.

# Jiang Yuying, Famous Professor at Beijing University, Who Daringly Rendered into Chinese the First Complete Walt Whitman

### 1

Yuying, you have more spontaneous sting in you
than all the hot pepper in Nepal.

### 2

The Red Guards humiliated your scholar husband
and he hanged himself
but when they beat you with a leather strap
one hundred times and shaved your head,
you turned loose a galloping horse of ice
in the hidden stadium of a crystal word.
You laughed at them.
How could they make *you* look like a Chinese nun?

### 3

You survive to tell China truths. Afraid? Was Whitman,
the boisterous fully contradictory Walt Whitman
in seed-picker outfit, a coward?
Whitman took the Fulton Street Ferry up to his bohemian bar,
Pfaffs, where he held court
or in his red shirt, open at the front, rode all over
his Manhattan on the open bus.
He kissed and wrote letters for a wounded soldier
in a Virginia hospital,
and nursed his slow brother Ed whom he lived with.
Yuying you are a friend
of the amorous freemouthed deviant who sang himself.

4

The Guards whipped your theologian father.
He was 86.
He carted his own bags down to the countryside
where they sent him to remold his mind.
It's too late, you say, what can they do now to you, an old lady?
(Yet why have I made up a name for you, Yuying?)


5

In bad years young fanatics always rise to denounce the wicked,
roaring slogans like their statued fathers,
yet, Yuying, you wait them out with humor.
You are loquacious
and candid on your own piece of grass
like the old bearded failure with his disciples
at his bedside.


6

Now, you have made Whitman Chinese,
that American gray saint who looks in the mirror
at his ravaged eyes and mouth.
Of course he gazes at you with satisfaction,
Mandarin Camarado, hurting, surviving,
soon for darkness and loth to depart,
and announces an end that shall lightly and joyfully meet its translation.
He sees the problematic poet who will die in 1892
in Camden, New Jersey,
a loner in his respectable poor man's room,
garrulous like you to the very last.

## Whitman's Grass

Walt Whitman, brother to brothers and brother to sisters,
intimate to intimates, keeper of free birds and animals,
acceding to worldly abandon and the freedom of the darkness,
Whitman, who foresaw a love that is given freely, asking nothing,
himself was asked, "What is the grass?" Or so a child spoke it,
and brought forth handfuls of the stuff, snatched from the earth.

We do not have to look in the poet's hands to know what grass is,
we do not look in books to read the cuneiform of the leaves,
nor enter the great libraries to deduce the signs of springtime.
Whitman studied the dark blades he had been given,
he saw the color green behind the color black, and saw, too,
a thousand sprouts unfolding from a single disposition.

There comes a time, in Whitman's flowing lifesong of himself,
a moment when the poet is at sixes and sevens, that very instant,
when the disposition of the writer springs in two directions,
thrusting one way toward death and dying, old age and eyes closing,
while in the other direction reaching toward eye-openings at birth,
and with each hand he clasps the other, making them siblings.

You, the reader, must locate this moment in *Leaves of Grass*,
you must pull the rug out from underneath democratic optimism,
you must stand on the bare earth and the bearded earth,
you must grant that the flag blowing in the wind leads to death,
you must, wishing to live forever, hear the poet arrest the wish,
and you must free mortality and immortality to be wed in the earth.

I am as fathomless as he, and you the manifest of eternal life,
I am the perceiver, and the receptor, of all he sees, as are you,
I am born of the smallest atom, and of the aggregate of atoms,
as you are that one whom he would have loved, as would I,
and I am he to whom the abstraction love takes form in the grass,
and to whom the word made flesh is as the rain on the field.

Walt Whitman, purveyor of unaccompanied journeys in the self,
star salesman of the constellations, of inner organs, of our ashes,
relentless believer in a universal scheme, yet hard at work,
I, a fellow islander, following you, echoing you, singing you,
preferring the organic to the inorganic, yet awed by the stellar,
throw you my casual salute and confide in you, and never ask.

# May 31, 1989

*May-be it is yourself now really ushering me to the true songs.*
— Walt Whitman, "Good-bye, My Fancy!"

It's Walt Whitman's birthday
so I should write a poem:

He'd be 170, maybe is
somewhere, better,
greyer than ever.
I like to think whenever I sense
lilacs, he senses them too,
when I view the moon hanging
half-an-hour high we both relive
the sweet hell within, children again,
once more.
I like to believe
I cannot sing a song myself
without him hearing it,
cannot cross into Brooklyn
or remember Rockaway Beach is
part of Paumanok, that fish-
shaped Long Island without
conjuring him up as real as
any other phantom on these
crowded streets, still,
sandy beaches.
I remember he asked me:
"Who knows but I am enjoying this?
Who knows, for all the distance, but I am as good as
looking at you now, for all you cannot see me?"
What a comfort, to believe eternity
need not dismantle death to maintain

its own integrity, what a comfort
to enjoy birthdays so many years
after we have said Good-
bye to our fancy.

# Whitman in Black

For my sins I live in the city of New York
Whitman's city lived in Melville's senses, urban inferno
Where love can stay for only a minute
Then has to go, to get some work done
Here the detective and the small-time criminal are one
& tho the cases get solved the machine continues to run
Big Town will wear you down
But it's only here you can turn around 360 degrees
And everything is clear from here at the center
To every point along the circle of horizon
Here you can see for miles & miles & miles
Be born again daily, die nightly for a change of style
Hear clearly here; see with affection; bleakly cultivate compassion
Whitman's walk unchanged after its fashion.

# Despair

It seems to be DARK all the time.
I have difficulty walking.
I can remember what to say to my seminar
but I don't know that I want to.

I said in a Song once: I am unusually tired.
I repeat that & increase it.
I'm vomiting.
I broke down today in the slow movement of K.365.

I certainly don't think I'll last much longer.
I wrote: 'There may be horribles.'
I increase that.
(I think she took her little breasts away.)

I am in love with my excellent baby.
Crackles! in darkness HOPE; & disappears.
Lost arts.
Vanishings.

Walt! We're downstairs,
even you don't comfort me
but I join your risk my dear friend & go with you.
There are no matches

Utter, His Father, one word

# This Night
## For Walt Whitman

How many years I have loved your poems!
Each poem is a curving stair of sound
And a barefooted dancer coming down.
You sing, my darling, like a dark rabbi
Among ocean herbs on the shore: "Night
Of the few large stars! Night of the winds!"
We wander for hours along the shore.
Go on. "Press close, bare-bosomed night."

## Camden, 1892

*Translated by Willis Barnstone*


The smell of coffee and of newspapers.
Sunday and its monotony. The morning,
Some allegoric verses are adorning
The glimpsed-at page, the vain pentameters
Of a contented colleague. The old man lies
Stretched out and white in his respectable
Poor man's room. Then lazily he fills
The weary mirror with his gaze. His eyes
See a face. Unsurprised he thinks: That face
Is me. With fumbling hand he reaches out
To touch the tangled beard and ravaged mouth.
The end is not far off. His voice declares:
I'm almost gone and yet my verses scan
Life and its splendor. I was Walt Whitman.

# Your Sister

*Do not cast me off in time of old age; forsake me not when my strength is spent.*
— Psalm 71:9.

For Ruth Roston

Walt, Walt, when you've a moment,
    come by the room of Ruth the poet,
gone from her spacious house, her garden
    with its ranks of roses,
(this day her birthday, also yours,
    she a mere eighty-one, and you
one hundred and eighty three),
    and as once you did with those young wounded,
who hollered to you as you entered —
    fresh-clothed, combed, your beard perfumed —
step into the silence of cut blooms
    where one sits with padded hands,
and wheelchair, and her shards of speech,
    come, old comrade, if you can,
from shadow, murmur some words,
    lay your lilac hand on her head
that's still like a lion's, kiss your sister.

# Canticle

Let others speak
of harps and
heavenly choirs

I've made my decision
to remain here
with the Earth

if the old grey poet felt he could turn and
live with the animals
why should I be too good
to stay and die with them

and the great road of the Milky Way
that Sky Trail my Abenaki ancestors
strode to the last Happy Home
does not answer my dreams

I do not believe
we go up to the sky
unless it is
to fall again
with the rain

# Early Evening

*These and all else were to me the same as they are to you. . . .*
— Walt Whitman, "Crossing Brooklyn Ferry"

Past the pedestrians, beyond exhausts
    of automobiles, above all the tall buildings,

a semi-translucent smear of clouds
    stretches across this skyline as if to embrace

Walt's city in its dinginess. Already
    bewildered by an early darkness, the fixed

stares of the automatic street lamps
    have begun; headlights flare down the avenues.

*What is it then between us?*
    the poet once asked, and his words lie tangled

this evening in my ever-darkening
    thoughts as those sharp angles of shadows

mutilate the Manhattan Whitman
    once knew. Piles of a special afternoon *Post*

headlining terrorist attacks — stacked
    so high between remaining morning editions

of the *News* and *Times* — still fill
    street-corner newsstands. A lone foghorn

sounds from somewhere farther
    along the East River. Construction workers

descend their scaffolding, skeletal
  metal glittering like glass under its string

of bare bulbs. A crescent moon arrives
  over the river, its worn image and waning

glow prematurely peering down
  onto the city's parcels, doing little to illuminate

the partial darkness of dusk, offering
  no comfort for the weary at this end of day.

# Small Acts

Whitman thought he could live with animals, they were
so placid and self-contained, not one of them dissatisfied.
I have lived with animals. They kept me up all night.
Not only tom cats on the prowl, and neurotic rats
behind my baseboards, scratching out a slim existence.
There were cattle next door in the butcher's pen,
great longhorns lowing in the dark. Their numbers had come up
and they knew it. I let their rough tongues lick my sorry palm.
Nothing else I could do for them, or they for me.

Walt can live with the animals. I'll take these vegetables on parade:
string-beans and cabbage heads and pea brains, who negotiate
a busy crosswalk and feel brilliant, the smallest act accomplished
no mean feat, each one guiding them to other small acts
that will add up, in time, to something like steady purpose.
They cling to this fate, clutch it along with their brownbag lunches:
none of us would choose it, but this is their portion, this moment,
then this one, then the next. Little as it is, pitiful as it seems,
this is what they were given, and they don't want to lose it.

The gawky and the slow, the motley and the misshapen . . .
What bliss to be walking in their midst as if I were one of them,
just ride this gentle wave of idiocy, forget those who profess
an interest in my welfare, look passing strangers in the eye
for something we might have in common, and be unconcerned if nothing's there.
And now we peek into a dark café, and now we mug at the waitress
whose feet are sore, whose smile makes up for the tacky carnations
and white uniform makes it easy to mistake her for a nurse,
even makes it necessary, given the state of the world.

And when the giant with three teeth harangues us to hurry up,
what comfort to know he's a friend, what pleasure to be agreeable,
small wonders of acquiescence, like obedient pets. Except animals
don't have our comic hope, witless as it is. They don't get
to wave madly at the waitress, as though conducting a symphony
of ecstatic expectations. If I turned and lived with animals
I'd only be a creature of habit, I'd go to where the food is
and the warmth. But I wouldn't get to say to my troubled friend,
"Your eyes are so beautiful. I could live in them."

# Walt Whitman at the Reburial of Poe

*. . . of the poets invited only Walt Whitman*
*attended.*
— Julian Symons

They got him in the end, of course.
In a polling booth, dead-drunk.
Vagrant, ballot-stuffer . . .
Four Baltimore coppers to carry that meager frame.
Our first detective of the broken heart,
he picked through its rubble
with his frenzied calculations,
his delirium of over-clarity,
until he found too many clues . . .
Once I dreamt of a man on a schooner,
compact and handsome, alone on the Sound,
thrilling to a violent storm,
threaded to this world by the silver
of a dying spider:
that man was Edgar.
He loved the moon, and the night-torch,
the notion of blood sea-temperatured
of the cold rush impelling him . . .
In life, in poetry, my antithesis —
detached from the true life,
of rivers and birds and swaying trees,
of soil red with tubers and pregnant clay,
detached from the wondrous release of sex,
his spleen beating heavier than his heart —
two or three men (at least)
packed in among a dozen demons.
He never much cared for my work.
I admired only a fraction of his.
But I happened to be in Washington

last night . . . and I'm old now, half-wise,
too old not to have a sixth sense —
for the genuine article, anyway . . .
I marvel at all he accomplished
in such a hatcheted life,
electrifying his losses,
celebrating the deer park, the potter's field,
as I celebrated forest and plain . . .
But then to finish here,
another half-forgotten city,
wearing another man's rags —
a scene he might have written:
streets snaking around him,
steaming and sulphurous,
rain dirty as it left the sky —
one last maze before the foothills of hell . . .
And that polling booth . . .
the drinking pals who dumped him there,
frightened perhaps by that dying wolf's voice;
it strikes me now, the eulogies concluded
(I wouldn't give one and I wouldn't say why),
how appropriate he should go that way,
how perversely American in the end —
a man who had consumed himself with exotica,
green as the Republic itself,
poet of our bloodied ankles and ashen
bones, our cankers and lurid dreams:
I wonder who he voted for.
I wonder if he won.

# Walt Whitman in New Orleans, 1848

It's spring, moisture's
everywhere, blotting its signature
into hatband and shirtsleeve, cooling
each humid breeze, trickling
down the wrist to soften my palms,
these old oaks steaming,
whiskered with moss and dew.

Dark skin glistens in gaslight
as I pass; satiny pastels, lips
puffy with what they've known,
the secrecy of carriages, stifling rooms
strewn with clothing, glassy stares
in dim doorways, men kneeling
before women as if in prayer, women
to men, to one another, celebrating
the rain and blood and need
bending us toward the sea breeze,
making us want to embrace
and move together forever.

At dusk, too many languages
and one language, scent of strange food
in pungent sauces, faint cries
and gasps of surprise — the world
aroused, all young men
old enough, waking suddenly
with something to say.

## Walt Whitman in Ohio

Walt Whitman has come to visit me in Ohio
I look at the beard of my old teacher and friend
like a gray spider web of rain
I look at his boots covered with American mud
         In two rocking chairs
         we sit out on the back porch
         exchanging words
Wherever he looks
         his gaze
causes the shoot of a poem to grow
*Where is your kosmos?* I ask him
*Where is the Western world one and inseparable?*
*the democracy? the eternal progress?*
Rain drips down from his eyelids
into the constellation of his beard
His shoulders bend
         under the invisible weight
*That's up to you,* he says calmly,
*I am expecting the main things from you.*

# Walt Whitman in the Car Lot, Repo or Used

Walt Whitman is wearing mirrored sunglasses
behind the wheel
of the buttercup yellow Mercury,
so that only when I see him do I see me.

I am in my black karate *gi*
not unlike the silk pajamas of my era,
and I'm late to the Center of Martial Arts
because my car is going to ash
in its heavenly naked body.

I don't want to think about the blistering Pontiac
that carried an actress to the river,
and leapt as she leapt, or the dreamboat
with perfume still on the dash.

Like any red-blooded American I lose the urge
to murder someone who oppresses me at every moment.
I think my pain is on another plaza,
and I want to sleep awhile, a day, a century.

But this dead man who looks in on me from the edge of my hammock.
What a burning angel he seeks and is,
swaggering toward each car trying hard to be a horse.
A drop of spittle in the shade.
a rose in the clenched teeth of a grille . . .

Time is a breeze that drowses in the sales banner
because he is not dead,
though he has died ten thousand times before,
on other shores where life was avoided.

The corpse of a car is mere manure
into which he steps unoffended
and shakes his white locks.

On the half-busted radio
he tunes a modern music,
an ashcan rant so I'll suspend my sleep
and sit shotgun,
looking for the hymn in the hymnal.

The butterflies in his beard are an explanation.
The gnats spinning around my head
a rendezvous. Every song he hears
he titles *Me*, until we look out,
then inward from the edge of the car lot,
as though it were our sea.

## Labor Day

all our jams are up,
& our watermelons, tomatoes, cukes & peaches.
cruising past these fields of corn,
their tassles shining in the sundown,
already I'm dreaming of Thanksgiving.
in fall l can't help but think of death,
what a dear color it is:
already here & there the maples turn;
here is a funeral cortege, holding up traffic,
the women covering their faces,
heads bent, the men solemn, staring straight ahead.
a whole life passes before me,
someone I never knew;
the sun shines over the hearse, thru the windows
onto their laps where their hands are folded.

home, sitting on the porch with you,
these sweet short moments
talking & looking over our marigolds
never come often enough.
yet together our lives're kind; we get by.
savoring this time
as the gardener puts his yard in order.
everywhere I look, people are whistling, busy:
now's the time to read Whitman again.

# February 12, 1865

February 12, 1865
To: Mr. Walter Whitman, c/o Paymaster
Office, Washington City

Dear Walt,

    The Cheyennes didn't get their lands.
Or food. Or justice. What they got was slaughtered.
Last November 29th. The governor sent out
Colonel Chivington and a regiment of Hundred Daysers
just to kill the ones that camped under our
protection down at Sandy Creek. Along
the way they managed to surround Fort Lyon, dragoon
the Colorado First and me. The colonel
cried for vengeance, said he'd string up any
son-of-a-bitch who'd bury their bodies or their bones,
quote unquote. It wasn't an army, it was
a mob. I flat refused to order in
my men or open fire. I soon found out
what's underneath that hide of Christian love.
That colonel-preacher went at me like I
was 666 itself. But I stuck fast.
Two days I testified before an Army board,
the colonel shouting challenges, the works. I thought
of you, and not without a smile. I mean,
here I am a soldier hectored by a colonel
just because I wouldn't fight. A preacher, who wanted
to kill the innocent, up against an infidel
who wouldn't. What do you make of that? Anyhow,
about a half the population want to kill me.

The other half are getting there. But some
Episcopals are showing signs of backbone and the Army's
on my side. Do I know what Quakers
must go through? Fraternal greetings.

Your friend,

Si

# Whitman
## The Wall

Washington, D.C.

I know this ground. I walked here once before,
alive. A septic smell, still. In this place,
tents, and my nursing, all through '64.
Or call it mothering. I looked in the face
of dying boy after boy. But now this black
winged wall, and other ghosts, their strange words:
Da Nang, Khe Sanh. But I know soldiers' talk.
And these dates. Sixteen years? Such a long war.
With the sun now come the living. A stream,
as if to board a ferry. Alone, or two,
a family, and all — they're reading the names.
Just that. America's great reading lesson.
I can be at home here. Mingle. Listen.
And lean against the wall, waiting for you.

# Whitman, Come Again to the Cities

*Burn high your fires, foundry chimneys!*
*Cast black shadows at nightfall!*
*Cast red and yellow light over the tops of the houses!*
— Walt Whitman

Father who found this vibrant light
rising out of the fired stomach of the city, rising out of
    the fecund genitals,
come with me
to the new sad cities
laid out on the earth like a tortured soldier,
the skin pulled off his back,
his eyes empty, but alive.
Come with me down the abandoned streets —
vacant lots of weeds, tin cans and blown garbage,
black and blue eyes of the windows,
thin dogs walking stealthily, a new breed neither wild
    nor tame,
but like those young boys walking with a starved eye
that deciphers quickly what can be eaten and what will eat.
What do they celebrate entering through metal doors
    to buy whiskey?
Mutilated seeds of the workers
through whose loins passes rusty blood,
and women who carry dead white ingots in their bellies.
Young men stand on street corners,
their clothes expensive, their cars impractical, wildly
    colored; and they will do anything but
put a piece
of another piece
in a certain place.

## Walt, the Wounded

The whole world was there, plucking their linen,
half-bald, mumbling, sucking on their moustache tips.
Broadway was still in business and they asked no favors.

All the cracked ribs of Fredericksburg,
the boys who held their tongues at Chancellorsville
as the bandages, mule shit, skin and shot

overran the Rappahannock's banks
and poured it in our mouths
that summer.

He sat up half the night reading to the Army of the Potomac
poems about trooping goats and crazy fathers
chewing grass in the wilderness.

   *It's me that saved his life, dear mother,*

   *he had dysentery, bronchitis, and something else*
   *the doctors couldn't properly diagnose.*
   *He's no different than the others.*

   *I bring them letter-paper,*
   *envelopes, oranges, tobacco, jellies,*
   *arrowroot, gingersnaps, and shinplasters.*

   *Last night I was lucky enough*
   *to have ice cream for them all*
   *and they love me each and every one.*

The early teachers stretched on canvas cots
with their bad grammar, backs smeared by caissons,
a heap of arms and legs junked beneath a tree

*about a load for a one-horse cart.* At night,
campfires peaked by shebangs in the bush.
He'd find the stagedrivers laid up there —

Broadway Joe, George Storms, Pop Rice, Handly Fish,
Old Elephant and his brother Young Elephant (who came later),
Yellow Joe, Julep Tarn, Tick Fin, and Patsy Dee —

the pinched khaki drifting down the gangways,
homecomers looking for those not waiting there,
bamboo lays and punji sticks alive in their dreams.

A small fire still burns in the nursery.
Rice and molasses simmer on the stove.
Children will have to learn to ask for less,

less from the elephant dawn that chilled
across the heights where Lee held his ground.
The sky curled its wrath about the land

and they brought America's fire home.
Fire on our hands, ashes at Bull Run, buckets from Pleiku
while he stood watching on the shore, pulling his beard.

> *America seems to me now, though only*
> *in her youth, but brought already here,*
> *feeble, bandaged, and bloody in hospital.*

Our roughed-up beauties dead or dying,
he sang them goodnight with his hands in his pockets
who would have kissed them and warmed their flesh forever.

When Oscar F. Wilbur asked if he enjoyed religion:
*Perhaps not, my dear, in the way you mean,*
*and yet may-be it is the same thing.*

To worship the fire in the nursery, fire in the hills
and in the mouths of those I love. I do know why
our wounded died.     I do know.     I know.

## Letter to Walt Whitman

Are you more than editions, or the grave's
uncondition'd hair? (More likely, these days,
permed and mowed to chemical perfection.)
I hope this finds you. I know you've been bothered

all century, poets lining up
to claim lineage. And not just poets —
in a photobook, brand-new,
handsome lads wrestle in sepia,

freshly laved by some historic stream:
the roughs are models now, and pose
in nothing on the opposite pages from stanzas
of your verse: a twentieth-century

letter to you. As are the scrawls
beneath the underpass, ruby and golden
cuneiform reinscribed on train-car sides:
songs of me and my troops, spray-painted

to our prophet, who enjoins us to follow
— what else? — our own lights,
intuitions glimmered in the body's
liquid meshes, our own

and the bodies beside us . . .
I am so far from you, Uncle, yet
in this way emboldened:
Last summer, in the year of our _____

nineteen hundred ninety-six, Paul and I
drove to Camden, where your house still stands
— modest, clapboard, dwarfed by the prison
glowering across the street, where trucks shock

themselves percussively on outrageous
potholes. Jail, detox, welfare: Camden
accepts it all, Camden's the hole in which
we throw anything, neighborhood so torched

it doesn't even have a restaurant.
You dwelt here, honored, half-confined, hailed
in your bed as a sage by a country
you helped to misunderstand you.

I get ahead of myself, Walt; the docent
unbolted the door to your manila rooms,
honey of June sun through shades the tint
of old newsprint: We loved the evidence of you,

fired by that filtering amber,
even while the swoops of car alarms
decibeled outside, and rips and crashes
by the curb made us sure our car'd

been stripped to the chassis.
Here your backpack, crumpled like a leather
sigh; a bit of your handwriting, framed;
a menu for a testimonial, and far too many

photos of your tomb: the stuff of image,
useless pomp in which you readily
partook — was this what we'd come to see?
Then one thing made you seem alive:

your parrot, Walt, friend of the last years,
a hand-span tall, lusters preserved
by the taxidermist's wax, or the case
in which he perched, or feathers' sheer

propensity to last. Your bird,
who ate from your own hand! And sat astride
your shoulder while you read the mail.
On whose bright eye's skim (glass now,

liquid original long lost to time)
curved this room, light through
— could they have been? — these shades,
while you crooked a finger to chuck

his ruffed neck. He's jaunty, brave,
his painted jungle gloamed in darkening
linseed, head crooked toward the future,
ambiguous as a construction by Cornell . . .

I thought if I leaned near that glass I bent,
patriarch, closer to you — he had
had your ear, didn't he, and if I leaned
toward his still-inquiring, precious eye . . .

I hardly heard the racket outside,
diminishing tremolo of sirens, names
the boys broke, laughing, as a bottle smashed:
I bent toward your glassed companion

still these ninety years in his sealed vitrine;
suddenly I seemed to see, tender, as if
I could smell it, Walt, powdered, warm,
the skin of your neck . . . Granted

this intimacy, I have some questions
for you. Did you mean it?
Democratic America joined by
delight in the beauty of boys,

especially working-class ones? I joke.
I know you meant adhesiveness,
that bond of flesh to equal flesh,
might be the bedrock of an order,

a compact founded on skin's durable,
knowable flame. I've felt what I think
you meant. I don't mean to romance this, Walt,
but much of what I've known of fellowship

I've apprehended in the basest church,
— where we're seldom dressed, and the affable
equality among worshippers is
sometimes like your democratic vista,

men held in common by our common skin.
But it doesn't take sex to understand:
once, in a beach side changing shed packed
with men, all girths and degrees of furred

and smooth, firm and softened, fish-belly
to warm rose to midnight's dimmest spaces
between stars, sunburnt on my bench, waiting
my turn in the mist of shower steam,

I thought, *We're all here, every one of us,*
the men of the world in the men's house, nude,
buffed with towels, young men and old
and boys bathing together, so much flesh

in one place it seemed to be of the soul . . .
As if I stood in that fogged, original room
through which each individual enters
the world, and each of us, nameless, already

in the body that would be ourselves,
was awaiting his turn. So we stood
in sympathy, since we understood
our fellows would suffer, knew

we were entering upon our singular,
shared lot . . . And I can understand
how you might base on that a nation,
Walt, though each of us left the warm

and darkened shed in separate clothes,
in separate cars, which drained out
of the parking lot onto the blacktop
and the expressway back to the city,

headed home to the song of my self, self,
self. That moment, unguarded,
skin to skin, why didn't it make us change?

---

. . . I have been interrupted here

by two Jehovah's Witnesses —
men in skinny neckwear with a boy in tow,
his dad's blond miniature — knocking
with millennial threats and promises.

I was not polite. Our poets fear
the didactic, the sweeping claim; we let
the televangelists and door-to-door
preachers talk hope and apocalypse

while we tend more private gardens. You saw
shattered soldier boys bound up in their beds,
lost your day job for writing scandalous
verse; you knew no one would base a world

upon what you believed: incendiary,
peculiar, nothing a "good gray poet"
could avow. Imagine being called *that*,
imagine *liking* it . . . Your little parrot's

ghost tweaks my ear, cautionary note:
How could I know the price you had to pay,
what you had to say to get away with
your astonishing news: no conflation,

you made it plain, to mistake the nipple
for the soul, souse of ejaculate
for the warm rain of heaven. It stops
my breath, to think of what you said.

How? You answer as the dead do.

———————————————————

I write you now from Columbus,
Ohio, the fourteenth floor, hotel tower
attached to a convention center

bland as a tomb, though the simile
lends a gravity actuality lacks:
acres of carpet, humming fluorescent tubes,
buoyed air, all of it waiting for someone

to sell somebody something. It's Sunday.
I'm a visiting poet here, currently
off duty. I'd like you to see my view:
candescent sky, fueled with orange plumes

and smudgings of a darkling plum,
one of Rothko's brooding visions
of what Moses heard, all spread over
the financial district of Columbus,

which just now I find strangely lovely.
Down there in the nearly vacant civic
plazas a few figures hurry against
a vicious spring wind, random Ohioans,

black sparks from an original flame. *Men
and women crowding fast in the streets, if
they are not flashes and specks . . .*

———————————————————————

And now I write from home, most of the day

gone. Paul's done the laundry, and downstairs
on the couch reads Proust. Soon we'll go out
for Vietnamese. We have what amounts
to marriage — sexy, serviceable, pleasant,

plain. You might have lived like this
awhile with Peter Doyle, who now can say?
Of our company in your century,
dust and silence almost all erase.

I wonder if you'd like those boys
in underpants looming huge on billboards
over Seventh Avenue? We're freer now,
and move from ghetto to turbid mainstream.

And — explain this to a ghost! — our theorists
question notions of identity: Are you who you love,
or can you dwell in categorical ambiguity?
Our numbers divide, merge and multiply;

shoulder to shoulder with our fellow folk,
who's to say just who anyone is? You
couldn't have imagined how many of us,
 — not just men who love men, I mean

all our uncountable specks and flares,
powerless, uncertain . . . You would not
like it here, despite the grassy persistence
of your name: I've crossed the Walt Whitman Bridge,

PA to Jersey, past Walt Whitman High,
even stopped on the Turnpike at
(denigration of our brightest hopes)
the Walt Whitman Service Area: shakes

and fries, the open freeway splitting what's left
of your American night, red sparks thrown
from semi windows arced in Independence Day
contrails . . . What could it mean,

for a vision to come true? Not
the child's-dream polychrome
of those Jehovah's Witness tracts —
happy people in sparkling nature,

a sparkling city welcoming. Poems
are written on the back of time,
inscriptions on the wrong side of a photograph:
scribbled flourish of our possibility.

Is it true then, what your descendant said,
that poetry makes nothing happen?
Just yesterday we worked in the garden,
earliest spring, brave sky, our apricot

newly burst into the first of seven
burning days. (When I saw a comet
from a plane, ancient tail a slurred flame,
it trailed these petals' icy double

through the midnight air.) We took off our shirts,
raked the dregs of leaves, glad for sun,
Uncle, while slender bees worried the blooms
in sun-buzzed endeavoring. We drove

to Fred Meyer, a sort of omnistore,
for saline solution, gym shorts, a rake.
In the big store's warmth and open embrace
who could I think of but you? We were

Americans there — working, corporate,
bikers, fancy wives, Hispanic ladies
with seriously loaded shopping carts,
one deftly accessorized crossdresser,

Indian kids in the ruins of their inheritance,
loading up on Easter candy, all of us standing,
khakis to jeans, in the bond of our common needs.
You wrote the book against which we are read.

*Every one that sleeps is beautiful.*
you said. Every one who shops is
also lovely: we go out together
to try on what the world is made of,

to accommodate all that bounty,
to praise and appraise, to see what's new.
As if to purchase were to celebrate.
*I stand close with the other shoppers*

*each in turn, I dream in my dream*
*all the dreams* . . . Who could be hopeful
for the sheer ascending numbers of us,
the poisoned sky and trees? Still I thought

of our apricot's upright, brandished flame,
scintillation held to the face of heaven,
new bees about their work
as though there'd never been a winter.

You answer me as the dead do.
And the poem stops here, Walt, while Paul
and I load the car with more than we ever
thought we'd need, white plastic bags flapping

in the breeze — the poem stops here,
in the parking lot, waiting for you.

# Centennial for Whitman

*(Amimetobion, not Synapothanumenon)*

I

What shall I say to Walt Whitman tonight?
Reading him here in the springtime of bursting green,
Foreign from him, held by the same air he breathed of the world,
Looking at night to the same stars, white and radiant,
Obsessed with a kindred obsession, at a dark depth,
Inheritor of his America maybe at its great height,

I praise him not in a loose form, not in outpouring,
Not in a positive acclamation of frenetic belief,
Not in the simplicity of a brotherhood, such peace,
And not in the dawn of an original compulsion,
But speak to him in the universe of birth and death.

By a Spring meadow I lay down by a river
And felt the wind play on my cheek. By the sunlight
On the water I felt the strangeness of the world.
Prone in the meadow by the side of the fast brook
I saw the trout shooting his shadow under the willow.

I sank into the mystical nature of memory
And became my beginning. I was one with strong nature,
At the heart of the world, with no need to penetrate her.
In the sheerness and the elegance of this feeling
I destroyed time and dwelled in eternal pleasure.

The vastness of the aim of human nature
Yielded to ease and immediacy of comprehension,
Such is the rarity of the mastery of existence
In the ethereal realm of pure intuition,
Within the subtlety of perfected spiritual balance.


II


What shall I say to Walt Whitman tonight?
Nothing that is not myself. Nothing for himself,
Who spoke the golden chords of a rough soul
Deep below the meeting of the mind
With reality; his words were a mask of the true soul.

I grew up among animal pleasures, hot in sense,
And fought off the lofty reaches of the intellect
As one knowing the soft touches of the night,
Running on the Spring freshets in delight,
Joyful and serene, not to be overcome or quelled.

Then dramatic evil like a blight overcame me,
The dream-like character of eternal knowledge
Was brought in earthly bondage; knowledge of death,
Our old enemy, appeared with his powerful will
And laid waste the garden of my green seeming.

The years began to whirl in a worldly ecstasy
Fulfilling some dark purpose confronting the heart
Of things, and I was loosened to flesh and mind,
Torn asunder from essential unity
And would wander the world in fateful duality.

This was the knowledge of good and evil,
This was the certainty of actual death,
The powerful hold of an ancient, fallen state,
The battering ram of time on the bones and eyes,
The new reality of the unredeemed mankind.

III

What shall I say to Walt Whitman tonight?
I look not upon the world of facts and figures
But in the heart of man. Ineradicable evil
Sits enthroned there, jealously guarding the place,
Only held at arm's length by a comic attitude.

Laughter at the sun and the moon, at the tides,
Laughter at the comedy of the eternal struggle,
And at the institutions and society of mankind
Laughter, I celebrate this tonic attitude,
And go as far as that for the sake of intellect.

And run on bitterness and corrosive pessimism
Standing under the glaring eye of antique satire
And range the fields of powerful condemnation
As one who allows himself such pleasures,
A beast engaged, knowing the gates of escape.

New bombs, new wars, new hatreds, new insecurities!
Man has become the victim of delusions
Thrashing his brains in energies of misaction,
Lost in tribal sin, ready to destroy himself,
Defenceless against all natures of monstrosity.

What shall I say to Walt Whitman tonight?
Give us a share of your love, your simplicity,
The large scope, the strong health of the soul,
Love be our guide, and love be our redemption,
Love make miracle, animate us now.

IV

Love come upon us when the willow bends,
Love come upon us at the child's upturned face,
Love recapture us in the market-place,
In churches, slums, on mountains, in the fog,
Love be with us in the hour of death.

Love be with us in the pang of birth,
And throw out hatred, envy, pride, despair,
Be joyful at the time of the tall daffodil,
Be rampant as the legendary lion,
Be meek and sweet, and sure, so love be here.

Love that is swift creator and saviour
Bless all the infants and the old men,
Bless the middle kingdom of the workers,
Love come in the soft night, in the sensual day,
Let our airs be soft flower-lofts of love.

What would you say to me, Walt Whitman, today?
Is there anything you can give me but your love,
That total devotion to comprehension of the word?
It is not the forms you evoked, these are changed,
But the force you spoke with, the heart's holy rapture,

Your knowledge of the changeless in birth and death,
The merit of man in his eternal suffering,
Your love of the stars, of valour, and of doom
That I would say to you, Walt Whitman, tonight,
That you could say to me, Walt Whitman, today.

# Walt, I Salute You!

From the Year Of Our Lord 19**,
from the Continent of the Amnesias,
from the back streets of Pittsburgh
from the little lit window in the attic
of my mind where I sit brooding and smoking
like a hot iron, Walt, I salute you!

Here we are. In Love! In a Poem!
Slouching toward rebirth in our hats and curls!
Walt, I'm just a woman, chaperoned, actual, vague, and hysterical.
Outwardly, my life is one of irreproachable tedium;
inside, like you, I am in my hydroelectric mode.
The infinite and abstract current of my description
launches itself at the weakling grass. Walt, everything I see I am!
Nothing is too small for my interest in it.
I am undone in the multiplication
of my perceptions. Mine is a life alive with the radioactivity
of its former lives.

I am in every dog and hairpin. They are me! I am you!
All is connected in the great seethe of seeing and being,
the great oceans and beaches of speeding and knowing.

I groan and surge, I long for hatches and engine sumps,
for sailors in undershirts. Walt! You have me by the throat!
Everywhere I turn you rise up insurmountable and near.

You have already been every Conestoga headed to California
that broke down in a cul-de-sac of cannibalism in the Rockies.
You have been every sprouting metropolis rerouted
through three generations of industrialists.
You, the sweat of their workers' brows! You, their hatred of poets!

You have been women! Women with white legs, women with black mustaches,
waitresses with their hands glued to their rags on the counter,
waitresses in Dacron who light up the room with their serious wattage.
Yes! You are magically filling up, like milk in a glass, the white
nylon uniform, the blocky shoes with their slab of rubber sole!
Your hair is a platinum helmet. At your breast, a bouquet of rayon violets.

And you have been places! You have been junkyards with their rusted Hoovers,
the pistils of wilted umbrellas.
And then, on the horizon (you have been the horizon!)
Walt, you are a whole small town erupting!
You are the drenched windows. The steaming gutters.
The streets black and slick as iron skillets.
The tawdry buildings. The rooms rented.
And now, in total hallucination and inhabitation, tired of being yourself —
Walt, the champ, the chump, the cheeky — you become me!
My every dark and slanderous thought. Walt, I salute you!
And therefore myself! In our enormous hats! In our huge mustaches!
We can't hide! We recognize ourselves!

# Another Nameless Prostitute
# Says the Man Is Innocent

For Mumia Abu-Jamal, Philadelphia, PA/Camden, NJ, April 1997

The board-blinded windows knew what happened;
the pavement sleepers of Philadelphia, groaning
in their ghost-infested sleep, knew what happened;
every black man blessed
with the gashed eyebrow of nightsticks
knew what happened;
even Walt Whitman knew what happened,
poet a century dead, keeping vigil
from the tomb on the other side of the bridge.

More than fifteen years ago,
the cataract stare of the cruiser's headlights,
the impossible angle of the bullet,
the tributaries and lakes of blood,
Officer Faulkner dead, suspect Mumia shot in the chest,
the witnesses who saw a gunman
running away, his heart and feet thudding.

The nameless prostitutes know,
hunched at the curb, their bare legs chilled.
Their faces squinted to see that night,
rouged with fading bruises. Now the faces fade.
Perhaps an eyewitness putrifies eyes open in a bed of soil,
or floats in the warm gulf stream of her addiction,
or hides from the fanged whispers of the police
in the tomb of Walt Whitman,
where the granite door is open
and fugitive slaves may rest.

Mumia: the Panther beret, the thinking dreadlocks,
dissident words that swarmed the microphone like a hive,
sharing meals with people named Africa,
calling out their names even after the police bombardment
that charred their black bodies.
So the governor has signed the death warrant.
The executioner's needle would flush the poison
down into Mumia's writing hand
so the fingers curl like a burned spider;
his calm questioning mouth would grow numb,
and everywhere radios sputter to silence, in his memory.

The veiled prostitutes are gone, gone to the segregated balcony of whores.
But the newspaper reports that another nameless prostitute
says the man is innocent, that she will testify at the next hearing.
Beyond the courthouse, a multitude of witnesses chants, prays,
shouts for his prison to collapse, a shack in a hurricane.

Mumia, if the last nameless prostitute
becomes an unraveling turban of steam,
if the judges' robes become clouds of ink
swirling like octopus deception,
if the shroud becomes your Amish quilt,
if your dreadlocks are snipped during autopsy,
then drift above the ruined RCA factory
that once birthed radios
to the tomb of Walt Whitman,
where the granite door is open
and fugitive slaves may rest.

# Green-Eyed Boy after Reading Whitman and Sandburg

Beyond the empty crossroads store
and the stubble of new-cut weeds,
a man in a rough shirt and wide straw hat
whistles me to a long morning walk.

Clean smell of hay. This joyful flesh.
The sweet sound of the hermit thrush.
A virgin river sings in my free-verse head.

Deep in the honeysuckle shade
we fish for our lost American souls.

Yes, I'm sure there's a place for me
in this knockabout, haphazard world.

Oh, but look how the summer wind
bends the branches of the sycamore trees.

A black dog howls behind the barn.

## To Walt Whitman

That old man — tramping down Flatbush Avenue —
with a cane, white beard, light-brown tunic
and gray felt trooper hat — that was you —
Walt — just like your picture — when you held court
in Camden — avuncular, garrulous, and ruddy —
I was climbing up the avenue — where it runs
between the zoo and the botanical gardens —
one of those "ample hills of Brooklyn" —
Why didn't I follow you? Why didn't I stop
and go back down with you? Something kept me in check
as I hiked toward the library — to finish my thesis
on you — You came to turn me around — there
you were — within a foot of me — here on the streets
we shared — and I missed what you showed me — You knew
that would happen — and encouraged me to look
for you again — that's what your beard proposed — I resisted
your very words I memorized — But missing you there —
I took the long way around to find you again —
In '91 — when I quit teaching — never to do a seminar
on you again — I ran to the barbershop to get rid
of my beard — which I hid behind since '67 —
Sitting on the big chair before the long mirror —
I saw my father's face — I came out from under my beard —

How do we change — Walt? Do you think poetry
has anything to do with it? Do you think we miss
our chance — the way I walked past you — until we
just get tired of the way we are — slowly ready
ourselves — and when that old man — I mean you —
comes back — find that we follow him? Say, the way you
went south — stopped writing editorials — visited the sick
in the city hospitals — owned up to those affections

churning in you — let out your fears of flesh-betrayals —
found your parallelisms and your lists and possessed your world —

I think of our lives — Walt — and they work something like this —
At Castle Garden — where you heard Jenny Lind sing —
and where my grandparents came through as immigrants —
I saw fishes in the tanks — sea horses with their plated
bodies — their beady eyes and crocodile snouts — standing
up in the sand — like curved musical notes — Tentacles
swayed around the mouths of anemones — and the tails
of fishes flicked as they disappeared in the caves —
I saw all this as a child — holding my father's hand —
We are connected — Walt — through that renovated round
building at the Battery — where I feared the glass
would break and all that sea life — and all that water —
come pouring out — drowning me — the fishes swimming
over me — out into the Upper Bay — through the Narrows —
beyond the mouth of the Hudson — deep into the Atlantic —

I think of our lives — Walt — and they work something like this —
I carried you around in my hip pocket — that old
Boni edition — the forest-green cover — leathery —
fitting snugly against my ass — I opened you up
on trolley cars buses ferries the el the subway —
Going to work — traveling to relatives — riding around
to escape my bedroom — I read about naked swimmers —
ants on stalks — splotches of moss and lichen — corpses
in the grass — oceans and pavements that spoke to you —
and that spoke to me the same — as if we were one ear —
I read you in my throat as the train made contact
with the third rail — the trolley with the overhead wire —
as the ferry with the accordion gate steamed to Hoboken —
O Walt — I convinced myself I absorbed you — that motion —
that parturient waiting — that sympathy — that listening
to bird, wave, and the grinder sharpening the knife —
But it took me years and years to get to my poem —
borrowing from you — where I recall I never kissed

my father — Even today when I walk the esplanade
at Brooklyn Heights I think of you and Hart Crane
and Melville — making up a past New York
that dwells in me — Once in '55 — during my lunch hour —
not far from the place where Lafayette kissed you when
you were a child — I searched out the corner of Fulton
and Cranberry — and there I saw the plaque on the wall —
above two garbage cans — marking the place — so it's said —
where you the journeyman set print for what you finally
called *Leaves of Grass* — book of voyages and retreats —
Back then I did not know that you could teach me
how to write out of my cave of despair — I couldn't see
how you had emerged — from the dark vaults of yourself —
Many times I missed you — though you were inches away —

I think of our lives — Walt — and they work something like this —
One high-school summer I cut and stacked steel piping —
and kept the green bins filled with screws — at Manny's
Hardware off the Bowery — where you went to the theater —
I walked under the el during my lunch hour and saw
how the fractured light linked with its own shadows —
how rails and ties and girders transformed the streets
to a chiaroscuro that spread to hoods and roofs of cars —
to the drunks wavering on the curbs — to the signs and pillars
of lights — to the green roofs over the subway steps —
Squares of pavements oddly glared in front of the dark
vestibule of a store — or where old-timers huddled at an entrance —
You — Walt — and Reginald Marsh and Berenice Abbott and Hopper
encouraged me to trust my hunch — that what I saw
in the colors and lines and angles of the streets —
in the arms of taxi meters — in the valleys of fedoras —
in the toe cleavages peeping from black pumps — in the lead
clamps that secured plates of glass where they met
at the edges — were recesses of myself — alphabets
to read — fractions of the streets and the shops
lodged in me — Mannahatta-tokens of myself —
Walt — it never dawned on me to walk east

60

and visit what was left of that Jewish world —
for it took me three decades more to walk *those* streets —
looking for the ghosts of Yiddish writers — entering
the remnants and renovations of their old haunts —
trying to imagine them there — Yet back in '47 —
when they were still in the flesh — I walked the other way —
So much so near — I never knew how to grasp — Your book —
Walt — I held it too close to me — and didn't even see
you warned against that — how that too was a trap —

I think of our lives — Walt — and they work something like this —
After the aquarium moved from the Battery
to Coney Island — where you raced up and down
on the sand — and declaimed Homer to the surf
and the seagulls — my kids and I looked at the brown
sheen on the seals — and the suction cups on the arms
of the octopus — A few blocks away my mother-in-law
was dying — depressed angry her life a waste — she said —
Refusing all help at the end — sliding back —
mumbling names no one — not even her husband — recognized —
she — and her world — went under — never to surface again —
Yet decades later my daughter named her daughter after
that old woman — and at the naming ceremony I read my poem
for my granddaughter — wondering what it's like to breast-feed
a child — even as I hit seventy and brood and nurse my back —

I think of our lives — Walt — and they work something like this

# Poem for Old Walt

SPRING DUSK DARK SHORE
LONG ISLAND NEW YORK APRIL
SKY OVER PATCHOGUE DENSE & GREY
AS WHITMAN'S BEARD
FLIGHTS OF GREY GEESE
NESTED IN IT
OVER HULK OF HIS FAIR BODY —
'FISH-SHAPE PAUMANOK' —
HULK OF HIM HOVE-TO
OFF OLD MANNAHATTA —
POETS STILL
SWIM OFF OF IT
THEIR FAR CRIES FAILING
LIKE LOST SAILORS IN A BURNING
TURNER SHIPWRECK
RED SUN FLAMES THROUGH
ON THE VERY SHORES OF LIGHT

# Reading Walt Whitman

I found his wool face, I went away
A crook; there were lines I followed
When his song like a whistle led me.

Daily my wooden words fell, a parade
Of sticks, a broom bent over a thief's
Head. But then along came Langston

The proper shepherd who sat on history
Missing our music, dividing me; after
His death I rewrote, I robbed, and hid

In a foxhole until my lines were wood
On top, and soft underneath the bark.
Good Langston sat too long to lift me.

# Walt Whitman at Timber Creek

*After an account by Justin Kaplan*

Twice the fangs strike your brain.
Your left side hangs stringless for a time,
your tongue lolls like a giraffe's.
Constellations drift paralyzed, silent
while you ride the pitch and grope of vertigo,
scrabbling for chairs, old certainties
snatched from reach by miscreant children.

By day a taut wire thrums in your head
at the comings and goings of vague shapes.
By night the ceaseless hiss of darkness
leaking from the room.

So you come to Timber Creek.
Behind the thick willow curtain,
stripped naked, you wallow
in the marl pit's mud.
With a stiff brush you rub
the grit like pumice into your skin.
You bathe in the creek's waters.

Fat, tanning, singing the name
of everything you meet
you dance your lame arabesques
to mullein blooms,
to dragonflies mated on the breeze.
Ringed by calamus, cattails,
you hear cicadas sing
of seventeen years buried
in the dark of earth

nestled to a root.
You wrestle saplings supple as boys,
feel their juices stir in you.
In the sweet grass you dream of Druids,
fall in love with the bodies of trees,
hear the wind's tongue
move from branch to branch.

It does not matter
that the hawk, stropped shadow,
circles omens
in the blue crown of sky.
The constellations
spin and sing once more
and the limp world comes firm again.

# A Story Having to Do with Walt Whitman

A friend of mine used to be, and still is, but only
legally, married to a dancer. The girl, this dancer,
his wife, had a teacher, one of those beautiful menschy
dancer men, who was dying of AIDS. He, the teacher,
as I imagine it, though it's not always true for dancers
in his company, had done nothing in his life but dance.
Well, that's perfectly enough. But the girl, this dancer, this
wife, who read as well as danced, thought she would bring him
*Leaves of Grass*, with the not inconsiderable presumption
that it would comfort him to the great end. (Presumptions need
not be false. It would have.) But this girl, the dancer, the wife,
once she realized that she had presumed, ascribing to her
gift and thus to herself a certain importance, worried
about it so much that she put off bringing it to him.

He lay at home and sometimes in the hospital, with
many friends in bright-colored clothes around him (they all used
to wear black and white, but thinking of death, they put on
rainbows). The girl, the wife, the dancer, worried and worried
about walking into the room of many colors. It
was not her wardrobe, she was not worried about that, though
she wore mostly grays, maroons, browns. She worried about
stepping forward in that crowd, having them look at her,
who did not even know if the dying man cared about her.
She worried she would be seen for what she was, not a friend,
but a pupil, and adorer. So he died and she
never brought the book. When she realized her foolishness,
as she always did, immediately after the moment
when it was too late, she just went down to the East River

and sat on a pier and looked at Manhattan and felt shame.
The book, a pretty hardback, in her lap. She sat and read
it, the whole thing. She thought several things as she read. One,
how can you die, not having read everything. Another,
how all actions should be as if for others, even if
none truly are. Three, how awful to die in the summer.
Four. She missed her husband, my friend. Five. She must work harder
at dancing. Six, what did it really matter if he
never read *Leaves of Grass*. Did it matter to the soul?
Seven, oh for goodness sake, what soul? The next day, she
agreed at his funeral to help clean out his
apartment. On his coffee table there was a Monet
with bad reproductions, Richardson's *Life of Picasso*,
Vol. 2 (the cubist years), autobiographies of

choreographers, and a battered paperback: *Leaves of
Grass*, what do you think? She opened it and found it all marked
up inside, with comments and all. Comments about how one could
make a dance with all this in mind. And she all of a
sudden remembered seeing the title "Afraid of the
Merge" on his list of choreography credits. Inside
the front cover it said "To my darling, from Gary." Instead
of this making this girl, the dancer, the wife laugh, or see the
humor in the whole thing, or at least see that she had read
him right, and picked the right gift, she just felt miserable.
This is why my friend and she had trouble getting along, for
he is not so complex and constipated as this girl, this
dancer, his wife. What happened? Oh, I expect she'll get over
it. Oh, one more thing. I am the girl, this dancer, this wife.

## Meeting the Master

> *I bequeath myself to the dirt to grow from the grass I love,*
> *If you want me again look for me under your boot-soles.*
> — Whitman, *Song of Myself*

well, there I was, trudgin' along to
class, yu' know, when all of a sudden
I felt this *squish*, like I'd just
stepped on some little soft-
boned, uh, mouse or somethin',
so I lifted up my left boot
and slowly peeled off this weird, uh —
well, sure enough, there he
was, a little teeny Walt
Whitman, flat as a
leaf of grass, only a lot
wider

# Memorials

Walt Whitman I lay on the grass today
outside the house where you were born
past International House of Pancakes
Whitman Jewelry Whitman Fences traffic
Within your unlatched gate it was quiet
but the doors were locked You were not home
At the center a grove of sugar maples
held dry buckets hung at their sides
and dry tap spiles Plastic trash barrels
spilled hamburger boxes onto the grass
I stretched nearby and imagined you
sliding bloody and surprised into West Hills Long Island
learning to walk across the wood floors
Around where you began spread circles
of citizens bargaining bearing ourselves
from automobile to marketplace
to bed to work and back again
Under our feet spread the smothered earth
In your yard the land breathed without hindrance
I held a familiar stranger's hand
We stood and looked in your windows postponing
departure over the gashed blacktopped meadow
Inside were a spinning wheel a set table
a hearth but not you Walt Whitman We
searched the grass and later each other for you

# I Love Old Whitman So

Youthful, caressing, boisterous, tender
Middle aged thoughtful, ten thousand noticings of shore ship or street,
workbench, forest, household or office, opera —
that conning his paper book again to read aloud to those few Chinese boys & girls
who know enough American tongue to ear his hand —
loath to select one leaf from another, loath to reject a sympathetic page
— a tavern boy's look, the stone prisoner's mustache-sweat, a prostitute in the sun,
        a garrulous old man waving goodbye on the stoop —
I skin *Leaves* beginning to end, this year in the Middle Kingdom,
marvel his swimmers huffing naked on the wave
and touched by his desperado farewell, "Who touches this book touches a man"
tip the hat on my skull
to the old soldier, old sailor, old writer, old homosexual, old Christ poet journeyman,
inspired in middle age to chaunt Eternity in Manhattan,
see the speckled snake & swelling orb earth vanish
after green seasons Civil War and years of snow
white hair.

# Lecturing on Walt Whitman and
# Emily Dickinson in China

*I celebrate myself*
*And what I assume you shall assume,*
*For every atom belonging to me as good belongs to you . . .*
There is no heat here.
The girl in front has ring worm of the scalp,
the shy man sitting by himself has fever-clouded eyes & a consumptive's cough,
but they are smiling. The Indonesian
beauty with one small black spot on her perfect
front tooth huddles with the others in the damp. Some
scrub Reeboks over the gritty floor
as I explain Walt's intricacies, stage his barbaric yawp. They ask
politely, why is Miss Dickinson
so concerned with heaven? A few have bound
their copies into books
with kittens and blue birds pasted on the covers.

Beyond the bars on the windows
one sees a boundless falling away
of palm trees broken bottles used kotex plastic and weeds
under a sky fat with the burgeoning rainy season.
Mosquitoes whiz and hurtle through the air. From the distance floats
klaxons of trucks, busses and cars cacophonious
near lunch hour as they barrel to Quinzhau,
narrowly missing walkers in straw hats, bicyclists,
pull motors lurching on the shoulders of the roads;
all things Chinese super-freighted with granite, cloth, wood, bricks and babies.
And above us, everywhere, speakers
rust on poles like low-tech idols. Cords snake & flap. I smile,
look into every eye as I explain
the uncertainties of life in 19th-century America

how the infinite could arrive in a virus, then unfold oppressive galaxies
where the only sound permitted was the buzzing of a fly, but a sudden bell
devours my voice
and all stand at once. Then
the speakers replace our private thoughts
with words large & tawdry as the billboards in the muddy fields.

# For Walt Whitman

Whatever it was to you,
    Finally I think I am only one blade of it,
        Tiny, infinitesimally

Also I think there is nothing very unusual about my life
    Or most people's:

Climbing the steepest face of the mountain
    Struggling to go up

Even as the dirty seesaw tips
    Slowly, irrevocably
        Down

Any one of the world's giants could step on me
    And never notice

Even if I cried out, in a cracked voice
    Under the rubble of the earthquake
        Among the dying cattle who would hear?

Not that there is anything so unextraordinary, either
    About my comings and goings:

It is just that there are so many of us,
    Each sword single,
        Each minuscule life . . .

Therefore to my mind it is more a matter
    Of quiet roots, of connections,

Of speaking out, loud
    Or just soft enough
        For a few friends to hear

The beautiful names of all those
    Who eventually will but must not
        Entirely disappear.

# The Poem of the Praises

*Tho' always unmarried I have had six children.*
— Walt Whitman

*No plausible claimant has ever come forward.*
— Justin Kaplan

My name isn't Lucius; I never grew up
to own the mill down at Spiritwood, where the falls makes the river a blue leg
slipping into the long white laces of a *danseuse*;
where the marl pit is, and the radiant amber and ember-red wildflowers
like powers, thrones and dominions putting on bearable form; I
never consolidated with Midas Mill Distribution, and contracted
later with Yancy Hobbs for the stream of half-price darkie sackers,
and later still negotiated the first use of the Edison illuminatory bulbs
in a 3-county area; and one day I didn't think of all the days,
and run into the meadow rubbing my face in the faces of flowers
like a rooting swine until someone came to speak carefully to me and carry me home.
My name isn't Rebecca; I never bore three children,
of which Matthew died of the yellow phlegm while still at my nipple,
but Columbine is a poetess of renown and my sweet Lionel Alexander
is the governor's aide; I didn't enter Henry's study
while he was at cards, and open the book of that jackanapes rascal
Darwin as Henry referred to him, and finish the book, and form
my own opinions; I didn't color my conversation with these
while serving the tea, for years, a deep brown veritable
Ganges of tea, and its steamy, pervasive weather; I never
bled, at my "time"; I never crocheted; I never rode Heat Lightnin'.
My name isn't Nathan Lee; I never gave up
seminary studies for astronomy — and that way traded heaven
for the sky; I never took as a lover the famous but stumbledrunk
opera tenor whose name I cannot here divulge, though he
and I like the stars were of the same mold and burning in affinity; and
at night in the observatory we never disported and wondered which
of the glass — the telescope lens leading high or the wine decanter going

increasingly low — could take a man farthest.

My name isn't Patience; I wasn't a stillbirth; I
wasn't even a stillbirth.

My name isn't Hamilton; and I was never ten; I never
gobbled grampa's Ladies Church League First Prize watermelon
entirely on the Fourth of July; and ran to the creek, to wash off; and
ran, I was as slick as a seed, and ran, past the burnt knoll, to the fields
where a mower whipped round at the charge of a wasp and his scythe
neatly severed my windpipe.

My name isn't Maysie; I wasn't released
at age 18 from the orphanage, to be a kerchiefed gypsy phrenologist
traveling with my monkey (Kip) and my body in bangles and taffeta,
a life of coins and kisses I would never trade to be a Queen; and
all the better for seeking out clues of my parentage, here
in a hedgerow, there in the chinese tea, wherever; I didn't find
my mother, a lovely colored woman the shade of a fawn's far underbelly,
of high rank in a Boston philanthropic society
dedicated to aiding her people, she had a room in a house
done up in sheaves of pressed African flowers and Mexican crucifixes,
and had that same excitement in her bones; I didn't find
my father, and who knows how many others' father, I didn't
approach an open window at dusk in that battlemarked slattern
of a house on Mickle Street, no; and if it happened, and
it didn't, I was 36 by then and he was ancient and ageless;
a candle was lit; he was writing; the hat he kept on was a crumpled
gray, the soft and shapeless gray of a dray-nag's muzzle,
his beard was that very color bleached by a shade; but the vase
was a fire of pinks and tiger lilies; he looked up from the page;
he didn't really see me, I could tell his eyes were still filled
with the page; and yet they said to me, *you are my child*; not
that it happened, it didn't; I left; a steady
current of people filled the street, alive and loud; his
eyes might have said it with just as much claim
to a hundred of them, in May, in Camden, New Jersey, in 1885.

And now we have read the books they write about our father,
singing his praises. This is the phrase they use: "singing his praises."
We, who never existed enough in his life, have read the singing
of the praises that never existed enough in his life, and now
from where we abide in the spaces between things touching, we
would like to sing his praises too. An antimatter chorus.
We would like to praise his words, they are so comely
in acceptance of the world with all of its rank perfume that sticks
in the creases and glazes over by morning, his words
that took the speech of horse-car conductors and walkup girls and
gave it the indigo-iridescent louse-ridden cosmos-connoitering
wings it deserves. We praise the ink of his words, it
is blacker and deeper than outer space though it fits in its
6-oz. crystal. And we praise the squid, that king
of all insomnia — whose ink glands mean perpetual night
is a living thing, tucked in its body. That king of diversion,
whose ink is a dummyself hanging credibly sized and shaped
in the waters — guardianangel-, golem-, doppelgänger-ink.
(And wasn't our father's ink his public being?) And
especially we praise the squid of the deep, we mean the *deep*,
where the waters are black and ink would be useless, but its
is a luminous cloud, a waft of bright light, a lamé.
(And wasn't our father's? Yes — wasn't our father's?) Now
a dozen squid are folded over a clothesline while the fishers finish
stacking their gear. We praise their knuckles a day's work's
rubbed dull garnet. We praise the air of the Greek islands over them
and in them, it has more dead than the air of some other places and
more honorable dead (we've seen our father open
Homer; marbled paper should be praised, and the raised
hubs of leatherbound spines). For every death filling the air, the lungs
have one accommodating alveólus, and this is efficient, fitting
synergy and cycling, so we praise the human body, every subatomic
pokerchip in the vast halls of its house rules. We
can never sing praises too many. Of even a rhizome, a protein,
one bulbette of roe. We have been waiting
in the null-spaces, here in the Byways of Possible Combination
one pi-meson wide, and we want to tell you those spaces are nothing

but genesis song. Sing with us. Simply be silent and
hear yourself sing. We are going to praise the almost-nothing
colors of malt and barley, in their barrels next to the dried green peas
and salt cod. We are going to sing for every string of sudden stiffening
below a nipple that flies it like a kite, for every wire
in a radio that's carried the news of murder in alternation
with the lyrics of love (doo-*wah*), for the life of the bottom-quark
(in trillionths of a second) and the life of the tortoise whose shell
time buffs to lustre its emerald burls over generations of men,
we're going to sing these praises and nothing can stop us, please
join in, we're going to sing of the perfect angle the beak of the
bluetit makes in territorial ardor, of the chipped hand
of a satyr on a bisque Pompeian vase, then of the chipped foot
of the maiden posed in flight, and how the signalman who's motioning
a jetliner into its bay is an eloquent stylized da Vinciesque figure
deserving of place in a pottery frieze for future archeological tweezers,
and of the moon, and of the nematode, and of the star-nosed mole,
and of the rumble of the moving van, and of the flash of a knife that
flashes other knives into the glare like one fish flicking
a whole silver school on its axis, and of a single scale in that school
distributing light's Newtonian range, of spare change
jiving in a pocket like an *a cappella* group in a basement club, the notes
they hit, and of the rose, and of the word *rose*,
and of the streetmarket bowl of roses on his writing-table this
otherwise grimed-over day in the late spring on Mickle Street, the book
he's writing, the room around a book or even a single poem
that's through now though the song itself, the cellsong
and the sunspotsong, is never through, and
we will sing the praises of you
and you will sing the praises of us, too.

78

# Whitman's Confession
## In the Cleft of Eternity

*. . . look for me under your boot-soles.*


What happened was my last breath fell back
on me like pins, the Ultimates —
and my hand slushed through
my chest into stars: None of you
mattered anymore, my nipples pointing off
the sawgrass and your faces all
dooryard. I did not wait for you long.
When the body was gone there was not even perfume.
There was a suck

like a choir about to and then not. I
tell you of the kosmos, vast puke
and scintillation. We do not go anywhere.
And when my eye studied
the catechism of the image it went: Worm,
nest, bridge, reflection, stripe rolling over
into worm. What happened was they

struck me with the bomb of the Buddha
all the multitudes from the top of my head and from
the ribs' shoelace. I withered firsthand, text,
translation, emanation, ink, and rag
into the cud of the Milky Way, thrush-
bone and mule-bone
wheeling in the dander-fields and through
the clean bowels of Orion
turning over me the blue straight-

hairs of the diamond. *Is this then a touch?*
What happened is I lost the animal of my likeness,
Earth of fur —
Earth of legitimate odors and of nights arm-in-arm.
I no longer know who set the woman on that road
or how her face can shape to what is missing.
I no longer know that the clasp of a man
is the cuttle of my vibrations.
Or that the lapidary of distances is memory —

Or that milk is cold.
You will not find me in any energy,
the tender, the gross, the metastasized, the skittish,
the thralling, the angelic. I hit the Void
running, and it was easy to betray you.
I could not wait for you. The poem
was the god who only yearned
to fuck alone.

## The Varied Carol

Whitman had no sirens to attend to,
*eee-you, eee-you* down the winter streets,
as in summer he heard no chainsaws or telephones,
no Harleys rumbling and spinning down gravel roads,
no canned laughter cascading from TVs
in neighbors' windows, no jet drone,
photocopier hum, stereo *ha-rumping* from
some highschooler's muscle car. He knew
no movie inferno roar, no jackhammer commotion
splitting a street, no squealing air brakes —
what great muteness to endure the world Whitman heard.

Yet I've forgotten a good anthology
of sounds he must have known like heartbeats homing:
*kop kop* of horse hooves over cobblestones,
the *chang* of one of their shoes on the anvil,
theater swelling with unamplified voice
of a diva, hubbub of a motorless street,
creak of well pulley, knock and slap of the bucket. . . .

But the sound he listened for best
is the same one I hear like a poplar breeze
following me wherever I go, and it is the sound
of hands in hands, of flesh on flesh, the dry
or moist slippage of belly across belly, lips on breast
or neck, sudden or languid sighs of peace being built.
And all whispered delicately enough by the weeds,
alive in the muffled rush of an owl's wings,
skittering like a strider across the skin
of a creek eddy. It is the sound of a cloud darkening

one half of a well remembered mountain,
defining the other side brilliant with sun,
and the sound of rain from a spout pooling
in the grass. The sound of a sparrow's feet scritching
across roof shingles, near the bed where all must sleep.

# Matthew Brady Speaks of Whitman

They are slowly emptying the Armory
Square Hospital. I will miss the smell
Of leather and manure the ambulances brought
To F Street each morning. I will not miss
The sawdust or the typhoid.
From my small studio I can see,
Above the cows grazing in the swamp
Of the west lawn, the completed dome
Of the Capitol. It sits like a lid
Placed atop the rumor and gossip
We depended on so heavily here.
It marks the end
Of a time when this city was mere *idea*
In the eyes of some. A time whose beginnings
I've filed in sections under lovely words
Like Antietam and Manassas; in portraits,
In all the chance moments
That will be labeled history.
Whitman? Yes . . . he was here.
I placed a hat on his head, had him smile,
And suggested he think for a moment
Of immortality. Forgive me, but he sat there
Like a gutted angel.

## Ghazal XXXIX

If you laid out all the limbs from the Civil War hospital
in Washington they would encircle the White House seven times.

Alaska cost two cents per acre net and when Seward
slept lightly he talked to his wife about ice.

My heart is Grant's for his bottle a day and his
foul mouth, his wife that weighed over five hundred pounds.

A hundred years later Walt Whitman often still
walks the length of the Potomac and on the water.

A child now sees it as a place for funerals and bags
of components beneath the senators' heads.

# Bread

I'm standing in elm shadow
   in the dooryard of a farmhouse
      on another star.
               It's long ago —

I know this from quiet all around me, only
   noiseless wind in trees whose toothed leaves
      now begin to fall,
               a few with each breath.

One slate step up to doorsill.
   I pass through to a hall. To my right,
      a woman in her kitchen
               with her small son.

She opens the oven. I breathe in,
   again, lung-deep, the hot
      ground-grain odor
               of rye flour. . . .

Twenty panes in each window behind her
   where the boy stands on a chair
      to look for his future.
               His eyes are lasers

probing fields I'd walked through to be here.
   He sees a city I now see
      that I hadn't seen,
               and now I know:

this is West Hills, Long Island,
    in 1821 or '22. Her husband built this home.
      She is Louisa Whitman.
                  I'm here in my dream

to see the boy whose words would be my bread.
    I hear him tell his mother something about the city.
      I already begin dissolving
                into my daylight body. . . .

As he said he did, he saw me, or saw through me,
    or stood inside me. Bread
      cooled on the table.
          I can almost

taste it, and will, until the Island's light
    opens into the breathing elms in time
      to place us there again
            where he was born, . . .

or when we dream, if this is true, we return,
    weightless, to worlds we thought we'd lost.
      We remember a distant city,
              bread's taste and odor,

but something from where we were,
    always there beneath elms on that other star,
      the one we wake in,
          now, here.

# Whitman Leaves the Boardwalk

I am so small walking on the beach
at night under the widening sky.
The wet sand quickens beneath my feet
and the waves thunder against the shore.

I am moving away from the boardwalk
with its colorful streamers of people
and the hotels with their blinking lights.
The wind sighs for hundreds of miles.

I am disappearing so far into the dark
I have vanished from sight.
I am a tiny seashell
that has secretly drifted ashore

and carries the sound of the ocean
surging through its body.
I am so small now no one can see me.
How can I be filled by such a vast love?

# Crossing Walt Whitman Bridge

Walt, my old classmates who write poems
Have written poems to you.
They find you, old fruit,

In the supermarket, California;
They hear you speaking from the brazen mouth
Of your statue on Bear Mountain

In poems, so many poems —
You are large, you can contain them.
From my Philadelphia suburb I drive across

Walt Whitman Bridge
Into the freedom of New Jersey,
Passing the Walt Whitman Bar & Grill,

Walt Whitman Auto Parts & Junk Yard, Whitman
Theatre, Whitman Motor Inn,
Your Pharmacy, your Package Store,

Your Body Shop,
And yes,
Your supermarket's really in New Jersey!

Past old bottles, fenders, corrugated shacks,
Your neon name on mirrored doors
And winos slumped across the stoops

Shadowed by the boarded thirteen-storey
Walt Whitman Hotel no longer glutted
With Americans who'd never read a line of yours,

Speeding now, I think of you
Ingesting science, scent of haybarns, daily news and country bunkum
To translate the Farmer's Almanac into a Jeremiad

And mix the sinner's Presbyterian dreams into your cockalorum
(You Nosey Parker, peeping through the transom
Of his relentless dream),

To make the murmuration of crowds
Into leaves of compassion —
What you spit out

Would keep all Europe
Civilized two thousand years!
What have you left but

A larger continent
Bulging to belch and yawp, lusting
For the nightwind's breast, the curled

Lascivious kisses
Of the frondy sea? Approaching
Mannahatta (it waits

Where the road dips far ahead
Beyond the toll-booths and the tunnel,
Spires rising to jostle the horizon

Over fumes and loud arrivals,
The press of crowds as in the old days)
I think of you — prodigious

Your digestion, swallowing
Democracy, not flinching from the secret
Shame exposed by torchlit nightmare,

The drowned swimmer and the battle-death —
All the heroes! Pocahantas too!
A letch for handsome draymen,

Ecstasy in capillaries
As in turning stars — How did you
Rise through itches from the bed

You and your idiot brother
Shared in a drunken
Father's house, your flabby body

Indolently moving
Toward the lightning's revelation,
Fecundity sanspareil!

It wasn't easier before the advent
Of a landscape gouged for money
Or the coming down of fallout

Than now after the dismantling
Of the brave *Bonne Homme Richard*
And the end of horsecars

To plant your seed
In Death's eyesocket
There to sprout in

Visionary life,
Always resurgent,
Never held down for long,

Felt alive,
Conceived and spoken,
So made true.

W

A

L

WHITMAN

Prophet of the body's

roving magnitude, he still

commands a hope elusive as the Jewish

savior — not dying, not yet born, but always

imminent: coming in a blaze one sunny afternoon,

defying winter, to everyone's distinct advantage, then going on

to Eden, half sham, half hearsay, like California or Miami golden.

All his life was squandered

in his poverty when he became

the body's prime reunionist, bankrupt

exploiter, from early middle age, of the nation's

largest    unexploited    enterprise — baggy,    queer,

a Johnny Appleseed freely planting selves the future mashes

into commonplaces, lops off as flourishes, an unweaned appetite.

Yet who can shape his mouth's

beard brimming bubble, that violent honey

sound? Afterwards,  they  just  blew  hard,

Tarzans hamming through the swampy lots.

His patent, never filed, was being man quixotically

alive against the hoax of sin and dying. Paradise is now.

America, whose greatest war was civil, must be born from Abel's wound

& Cain can be welcomed home

by Adam — Father Abraham

opening his blood to continents,

all armies, lovers, tramps. A time for heroes, but

the captains, shot or dowdy, died. (Had old Abe really smiled

& tipped his hat or had he merely grimaced?) Ulysses, finished, promptly

sighed & chomped cigars & toured the capitals. The people yea'd & shambled

to the great fortunes

made, while he conveyed the lippy

cop, the whistling streetcar man, the ferry

pilot billowing  upon  the  apron  of  his  praise.

Nakedly    at    last    he    flailed    his    own    paralysis

with mud & flesh-brush. A man, all men, himself alone, a rugged blue-

eyed testament, his looks in Brady's lens are calm with after-rages.

"The      real      war

will      never      get

in      the      books."

Below the ragged

line  he  signed

his chummy name.

# Whitman in a Corner

*The house is a sort of airy structure that moves*
*about on the breath of time.*
— Gaston Bachelard

The graying poet of Camden
sits where two walls meet,
afraid of light and sound
as it comes in the window:
the hearty noise of children playing
and women calling out to their mates
as they trudge home from work.
The poet of the out-of-doors
faces the closet safely,
watching a spider tread its web
as if in a boundary house.
The metaphysics of open places
drags at him like God,
who knows the names of everything
but only dumbly points.
To find oneself in the open,
outside the house of breath,
is to lose yourself in the world.
Therefore, he sits in a corner,
where memory falls into the present,
inhabiting nothing but simply being
with rudely cosmic force.
But when he does his writing
in a dark, containable room,
these things take on their mortal stain,
blooming with particular force
into the shapes they are.

When Oscar Wilde comes to call,
the two men sit in his crowded study,
knees together, laughing.
And when Walt Whitman plans his tomb,
it's not a simple grave
where the outside can obtrude,
but a stark black mausoleum
with eaves and cornices,
as if even in death
he couldn't leave his house.

## Old Walt

Old Walt Whitman
Went finding and seeking,
Finding less than sought
Seeking more than found,
Every detail minding
Of the seeking or the finding.

Pleasured equally
In seeking as in finding,
Each detail minding,
Old Walt went seeking
And finding.

# Walt Whitman in Hell

*. . . on the black waters of Lethe?*
— Ginsberg

In the second circle — the level of perpetual dysfunction
Where untouchable lovers are damned by definition
To read each others' stories over and over

In voices like monotonous tape loops repeating forever
The lessons of the *Book of the Unabridged Living Body* —
The interior lights of a downtown express strobe

Grand Central platform and vanish, leaving nothing
But a retinal afterglow of the Lexington Avenue line.
Engines push tarry winds out of the heavy darkness

Of the tunnels. They break like punished hurricanes
Into the station's wintery light. I carry a map
Of this place in memory only — uptown, downtown,

Crosstown — capillaried in the visual mind,
Terminal names a systole and diastole of space
That contracts and relaxes around me when I think of it,

Including everything, the whole corporeal ghost
Of Manhattan and beyond. But where is anything, really?
Do I dare trust memory's directions? Or is this the first

And most damning despair, that it all may be nothing
But dots, biochemical flashes, swampgas waverings
Of imaginary light, the meaning of this landscape

Of ashes simply being that I have to wonder
What it means, and thereby recall myself?
And as if this uncertainty were one of the most sublime

Angels of torture, I am suddenly empowered
To remember the mountains, hills, and gorges
Of Manhattan, where the gates of the subways appear

To the sight like holes and clefts in the rocks,
Some extended and wide, some straitened
And narrow, many of them rugged — they all,

When looked into, appear dark and dusky;
But the spirits in them are in such a luminosity
As arises from burning coals. Someone

Among them plays a saxophone — no, someone scats
A bebop riff in a voice so skewed by sterno
It comes through sounding like brass,

And modulates into the Lydian mode:
Someone of them remembers *A Love Supreme*,
And this is my signal, I go down, and everything begins.

It is given now that I realize what comes first,
The station of instruction, the 81st Street entrance
On the Avenue of the Americas line. I enter

From the basement of the Museum of Natural History,
Where passing over is a simple fact, no astonishment,
Because overhead is a whole granite houseful

Of *memento mori* — tombstones, mummies,
And the icthysaur's whatmeworry grin. The way here
Is wide and smooth, passing over is a token

I buy from a woman in a Plexiglass cube,
Passing over is a slot and the click of a turnstile. It is here
The man with the methyl voice sings Coltrane and passes out

Pamphlets enumerating the seven words that mean
*The body thinking: Thumos, Phrenes, Nöos,* and *Psyche,*
All of them translated variously from Homeric Greek

As *mind* or *soul* — and *Kradie, Ker,* and *Etor,*
Rendered often as *heart* or *spirit.* But all
The translations are wrong, I read, entirely:

These must be thought of as objective parts
Of the body, the pamphlet tells me, understood
As my first clue that I am leaving

Anything behind. I embody now the plains and valleys
Of Brooklyn near the foot of the Brooklyn Bridge,
Where the subway gates resemble dens and caverns,

Chasms and whirlpools, bogs, standing water —
And when they are opened, there bursts from them
Something like the fire and smoke that is seen in the air

From burning buildings, or like a flame without smoke,
Or like soot such as comes from an explosive chimney,
Or like a mist and thick cloud: it is here the woman

With a face like a drowned suicide's crouches
At the first turning of the downward stairway
I can't help choosing, holding up her autocratic

Homemade sign: I AM A VICTIM
OF THE CONSPIRACIES OF NAZI RACIST
HATRED THEY HAVE SEALED MY VAGINA

WITH MOLTEN LEAD AND LEFT ME TO DIE
ALONE THEY SEND MY CHILDREN BACK TO ME
DAILY IN MANILA LEGAL ENVELOPES

PIECE BY MYSTERIOUS PIECE DON'T BELIEVE
A WORD THEY TELL YOU PITY ME.
It is here I feel the first angina constriction

Deep in the cardiac mind, and the Nöos says to the Psyche,
*Watch where you go once you have entered here,*
*Which way and to whom you turn,*

To which the Kradie answers, *That is not our concern.*
*It is our fate to open every door.* So I remember, now,
This is the real truth of it: I enter from every gate

At once, on every numbered street and avenue,
Jackson Heights, Mount Eden, Bleeker, Lorimer, 59th —
And the enormity of my multitudinousness,

This apocalyptic rush hour, eclipses even the brilliance
Of the four quarters of the midnight city —
Regions with designations, attributes, and enumerations:

*North* the Quarter of the Vomiting Multitudes,
*East* the Quarter of Suppurations, *West*
The Quarter of the Pissing Millions, *South* the Quarter

Of Investment Banking — but before I can say them,
The great fluid weight of my entering
Washes me forward, and the silent electric doors

Of the silver cars open all together to take me in,
Every human soul of me at every intersection
In every borough of the city, bringing me in a thunderous

Convergence of superimposed switch engines
Simultaneously *here*, to a level that demands me,
Grand Central Terminal, and the carriers disgorge me

In my statistical millions to circle
From platform to platform where the right trains
Never come. Every man and woman who was breathing

An instant ago must be with me now. Here is the tourist
From Michigan; she was staring at the Empire State
When a cloud of noxious oblivion touched her,

And she opened her eyes and was part of me.
Here is the lawyer from Queens; he knew the city
Inside out, but now he wanders this station

He passed through hundreds of times in his life
Wide-eyed and blank, dangling his forgotten briefcase
Like the ghost of a severed limb. Here is the man

Who bewildered, here is the child who devoured,
Here is the old Hindu woman who lived
Sweetly as a saint, and woke to this at ninety

From a heart-bursting sexual dream, the perfect
Circle of the caste mark between her eyes
Red as a cartoon bullet hole.

Here is the stockbroker, here is the stewardess,
Here is the crowd of girls with prep school sweaters
And halos of frosted hair who seem to be joined at the waist.

Here is the Chinese couple who juggled feathers
At the Lincoln Center circus — they move
Their disciplined hands together, seeking a familiar balance.

Here is the Chilean ex-diplomat who went in fear
Of CIA assassins — to him these tiled walls
Have a beautiful coolness, he's never been so calm.

Here is the defrocked priest: forgetfulness
Has utterly altered him. Here is the ex-Reagan aide:
She seems completely unchanged.

And the Priestess of Greenwich Village,
And the slacker, and the dental assistant,
The majorette, the machinist, the freak, and the mother's son —

This is more than consent, or concord; it is a real
Unity of us all, in one and the same person,
Made by covenant of all of us with each of us, in such a manner

As if each of us should say to all of us, I *Authorize*:
I am a random human diorama, an outtake
From *The Night of the Living Dead*. This is my punishment

For forgetting to believe that blankness is the logical
Outcome of my passionate confusions. Now chaos darkens
The holy brightness of the unconscious world.

Overhead, signs light up to enumerate directions and destinations:
*A Lake of Fire. A Bottomless Pit. A Horrible Tempest.*
*Everlasting Burnings. A Furnace of Fire. A Devouring Fire.*

*A Prison. A Place of Torments. A Place of Everlasting*
*Punishment. A Place Where People Pray. A Place*
*Where They Scream for Mercy. A Place Where They Wail.*

*A Place Where They Curse God.* In the vastnesses
Of Sotheby's, snuffboxes, folk arts, antiquities, toys,
Judaica, and other sacred artifacts take on

An unearthly luminosity — at the Village Gate,
The horns of fusion musicians synthesize and burn.
Now the imperious *Phrenes* begins

To thrash far down in the shadows of the diaphragm,
The intercostal muscles of the rib cage, the smooth
Muscles surrounding the bronchial tubes

Which regulate their bore, and so their resistance
To the passage of air — and beside it, or within it,
Its Siamese-twin dopplegänger image or other self,

The terrible *Thumos*, also snorts out of a primitive dream
Of breath-souls and the smooth interiors
Of ventricles and veins, black bile and yellow bile, mucous

And vitreous humors. They surface together
Like incestuous homoerotic lovers waking hours
Before sunrise, both blind and invisible,

Caught in a bedroom-darkness so profound
They might be sealed in the flesh-insulated cavity
Of one enormous torso. They begin their old dialogue,

The equivalent of the talk of husbands and wives —
*Did you hear a noise? Did you take out the garbage?*
*Did you pay the gas bill? Are the children murdered?* —

But spoken in something other than words,
Whatever the language of nerves and corpuscles
Consists of, which cannot be rendered in the syntax

Of consciousness, but whose faintest echo
Translates roughly [Phrenes] *If the body vanishes,*
*How can the spirit be broken?* [Thumos] *Don't ask.*

Its scars leave residues. [Phrenes] But if it is the body
Which breaks, how long does it take for the heartbeat
To calcify? [Thumos] Hush. Tell me the story

Of the place breath goes to survive
The suffocations we make for it. [Phrenes] It is a place
Where they can never repent, a place of weeping,

A place of sorrows, a place of outer darkness,
A place where they have no rest, a place of blackness
Or darkness forever, a place where their worm dieth not,

And fire is not quenched. [Thumos] And none of this is certain?
But nobody answers, for now the darkness modulates,
And I find I am in a space exterior to the body after all,

On a secret path along the rim of the starless city, perhaps,
Between the wall and the torments, or perhaps in a tunnel
Dug far below the other shafts, where I have been

Let down through a column that seems of brass,
Descended safely among the unhappy that I might witness
The vastation of souls. A multitude of pitiful

Men and women are gargoyled by homelessness here,
Hung in various ways by the different parts of themselves
Corresponding to the sociology of their births.

And the Thumos says to the Phrenes: Enumerate
The ways the human body can be warped
By punishments, political or metapolitical, and how

Those punishments make allegories of suffering.
Do so succinctly, in an orderly way, clearly,
And giving examples. And the Phrenes offers up

This answer: *These are the measure for measure*
*Hanging retributions against the disenfranchised:*
*Those who are Guilty of Passion*

*Or Cleanliness shall be hung by the pubic hair;*
*They shall be hung by the pierced thighs, Those*
*Who are Guilty of Standing Erect; by the eyes,*

*Those who have Seen Things Clearly; by the nose*
*Those who Smell the Death of the Rat in the Wall;*
*Those Convicted of Worthiness shall be hoisted*

*By the reputation; Those Convicted of Intelligence*
*By the delicate inner skin of the wallet; by the tongue*
*Those who Know Poverty, Hunger, Color, or Charm;*

*By the ears Those who Learn the Direction*
*Of the Class Dialectic; by the genitals Those*
*Refused Credit; by the breasts Those Discovered*

*Suckling More of Their Own Kind; by the DNA,*
*Those who Combine Unfitness with Survival;*
*By the Phrenes, the Ones who are Poor and Disbelieve;*

*By the Thumos, the Ones who are Poor and Believe.*
From the safety of my vantage point, I see
The truth of it all. The damned are ranged

Before me, row on blighted row. I approach the first
Prisoner or corpse or dead soul, a man dangled
By the tissues of the soft palate for the felony

Of his native tongue — he is effigied in the black rags
Of an ancient uniform of the Ohio National Guard,
His empty eye sockets ringed with kohl and stuffed

With planted Columbian Gold, the parchment
Of his forehead tattooed with the nine mystical numerals
Of the cabbala of Social Security

And the Kent State coat of arms. In horror
Of this blasphemous apparition, I fall back,
Nearly fainting, and stagger into a landscape

Where five hundred thousand blasted acres
Have been ripped apart by trenches and shells,
Villages cast down in ruins as if by earthquake,

Wounded trees, limbless and headless, looming
Above the desolation like scaffolds, the valley
A skeleton without flesh, save for the bodies

Of half a million dead ground up beneath the ceaseless
Bombardments. In insensible confusion, I stumble
On the misery of women moaning in parlors, in memory

Of the names of rivers their husbands died for —
The Nile, the Rhone, the Rhine, the Somme, the Marne,
The Aisne, the Yser, the Meuse, the Chicamauga,

The Yangtze, the Mekong, the Tigris and the Euphrates,
Where stealth bombers and F-111s vomit sulphur and acid
On the Mesopotamian plain until the image of my old father

Gilgamesh lurches out of the dust to lay hands on
The byzantine levers of a T-72 Soviet tank.
One of these demons of unforgetting, a magnetized girl of twenty

Who lived sixty years beyond the day of her lover's desertion
By fuel-air bomb in the wreckage of Panama City,
Comes forward to comfort me with bandages and morphine,

Cool hands on the brow. The story of her girlhood
Materializes within me, an immaculate marriage
Of nightmare and menses. Now the voices of my stillborn

Sons and daughters rise from the blistered tarmac,
The strangled books of the vanished poets
Of America — Lindsay, yes, and Sandburg, my binary idiot clones,

But louder I hear sweet Edwin Rolfe, whom no one now remembers:
*John's deathbed is a curious affair,* he is singing,
*The posts are made of bone, the spring of nerves,*

*The mattress bleeding flesh. Infinite air,*
*Compressed from dizzy altitudes, now serves*
*His skullface as a pillow.* In my drugged fever dream,

I am damned to the furious realm of Sol Funaroff, where
*The earth smoked and baked; / stones in the field*
*Marked the dead land: coins taxing the earth —*

And to Countee Cullen's crucifixion:
*"Maybe God thinks such things are right."*
*"Maybe God never thinks at all . . ."*

It seems the body is scattered over the whole expanse
Of thought, arms and legs sliced away and dropped
Horribly into a pail, the circuitry of the nerves

Corroded, abdominal cavity looted for spare parts
And salvage, the *Kradie* and the *Ker*
At infinite removes from one another,

The *Psyche* bereft of the *Etor* — body and body politic
Forever dissevered, like precincts of the brain
In the wake of a bad lobotomy. I try to remember

Wholeness, the image of meadows in starlight,
Lovers in sentimental landscapes, glacier-capped
Purple-skewed mountains, the visionary wheathead

Held up by the Dionysian priest at Eleusis,
The imperious cliché of the sea, the splendid material love
Of Rukeyser — *I have gained mastery*

*Over my heart / I have gained mastery*
*Over my two hands / I have gained mastery*
*Over the waters / I have gained mastery*

*Over the river* — but it splinters in a billion diffractions,
Cells, dustmotes, atoms of asthmatic pollen,
Spume, sperm, fragments of quartzite, nitrogen,

Duct tape, cotter pins, subatomic wreckage,
Shreds of pointless false narratives left over
From childhood memories or from moon-illumined

Bedrooms where lovers defected from one another's countries.
This is the critical whirlwind. Nothing holds here.
I fracture again and again, giving in to every mythology.

The shattered ghosts come thick. Submicroscopic,
I seep through cracks in the nuclei,
An insidious multitudinous radioactive dust,

Undetectable by any instrument except as an oscillation
The cosmos emits at its own dismemberment
Into particles, into bodies carrying bowls of goats' blood,

Each going down into the hell of its own one-track mind.
Here is the ruptured anarchist soul
Of Arturo Giovanetti in prison, the one true confession

Of his poetry: *Wonderful is the supreme wisdom of the jail*
*That makes all think the same thought. | Marvelous*
*Is the providence of the law that equalizes all, even*

*In mind and sentiment. | Fallen is the last barrier of privilege,*
*The aristocracy of the intellect. | I, who have never killed,*
*Think like the murderer; | I, who have never stolen, reason*

*Like the thief.* What is this place where wisdom
Is an unnatural abomination, all knowledge is nature
Destroyed? How have I come to this perigee, where the heart is nothing

But a spring, and the nerves but so many strings,
And the joints but so many wheels, giving motion
To the whole, as was intended by the artificer?

Here the larynx of Mike Gold, dipped in solder
And traced with magnificent circuitry, picks up the broadcast
His own crushed poems repeat into the emptiness

Like a satellite beacon: *I am resigning from the American Legion*
*It reminds me of a dog I used to have*
*That picked up toads in her mouth. . . .*

Now, as the voices of these my emanations bark and bleed,
It is the intense strangeness of the world I want
To remember how to love — how it enters and exits

The body, air and ether and light — and to which I long
To return, thrown into being out of the center of being.
But what am I — an insulated ghost, appearance, apparition,

Epiphenomenon, holographic projection,
A comic book death's-head cast up on the shore
Of the living? Even this skin, which once trembled

At the thought of the touch of another human body,
Is unreal, only the projection of a vanished surface:
And the mind, when it falters and croaks —

I speak with authority now — loses its shape
As a bodily ego, follows the carcass
Cell by carrion cell, down through vegetable ooze

And crust and maggoty mantle and magma,
And arrives, in the innermost circle
Of the Republic of the Disappeared, at emptiness.

It was here, in the Land of the Metaphysically Free,
That, fallen, I dreamed my old America. By an act
Of most imperial will I assumed the Presidency of the Dead,

I shaped the ruptured shrapnel of my consciousness
Once more into a seedy mercenary army —
*Phrenes* and *Thumos* and *Nŏos*

Commanding rank and file of the husks
Of riveters and lawyers (I gathered them
Tenderly as they settled), and residues of secretaries,

Dregs of ushers, gynecologists, thieves,
And the fine ash of Iraqi cabdrivers,
And the delicate grit of Marines,

Dust of Bush, Baker, Schwartzkopf, Cheney,
And beautiful Colin Powell: such a clay they made,
Such a multitude molded, such drum-taps and battle hymns.

At last I believed I understood them. At last
When I called their names they seemed
To shiver to hear me, as if they were almost alive.

But when I look now, there is only the finitude
Of nothing, only absence. I stand in the ultimate circle,
The innermost hell of all the hells, beyond

The outermost illusion: Purity, uncorrupted
Conscience, the body politic embracing
Self and nothing other, only the singular desire.

And as if at a mystical chime, or the alarm
Of a mineral clock, the subway signals ring again,
And I rush at the speed of darkness

From station to station, through the gnarly strata,
In among the tunnels of volcanic roots and sealed absolutes
Of salt domes, up along the nether edges

Of the limbo of Flushing, transformed at Queensboro Plaza
And again at Hoyt-Schermerhorn, to emerge at last
In mercuric February afternoon light

At the stairway marked *Brooklyn Bridge*.
Nothing has changed. Manhattan grinds on,
Gears of the living irreversibly meshed

With the ratchet of desire. There is still the apocalyptic
Discharge of cluster-bombs over the lower east side,
Brimstone of artillery out of the Village, sniper fire

From the Chrysler Building, the strafing
Of Bloomingdales. But everything on the earth I love
Is sealed from my touch as by a zone

Of Platonic plate glass. In my loneliness I rise
And hover over the plutonium-gray span
Of East River, licked by the harrowing fallout

Of my own intangibility. From here I can see,
Like a skyline, the obvious contour of all
My error. O I freely confess it now: America,

I was wrong. I am only slightly larger than life.
I contain mere conspiracies. What do I know?
There is no identity at the basis of things, no one

Name beneath all names. There is no more than this
To remember: *It is not godlike to die. It is not even human.*
*Refuse the honor, no matter who tells you its conquest is sublime.*

I may have mumbled that old lie myself once.
I have confessed to many things. Maybe that is why I am
The only one dead here. Maybe that is why I have to suffer

Everything I can. Maybe that is why —
Over the unconscious roofs of your living
Beauty shops, sweatshops, pawnshops, printshops, meat shops,

Warehouses, bathhouses, crackhouses, penthouses, card houses —
Once and for all unhearable, and for all I know unthinkable, I go on
Sounding my doomed eternal bodiless goddamned

I, I, I, I, I.

# Walt Whitman in the Civil War Hospitals

Prescient, my hands soothing
their foreheads, by my love
I earn them. In their presence
I am wretched as death. They smile
to me of love. They cheer me
and I smile. These are stones
in the catapulting world;
they fly, bury themselves in flesh,
in a wall, in earth; in midair
break against each other
and are without sound.
I sent them catapulting.
They outflew my voice
towards vacant spaces,
but I have called them farther,
to the stillness beyond,
to death which I have praised.

# Under the Sign of Walt Whitman

Whitman would have admired Willimantic's
4th of July Boombox Parade, the most democratic
parade in America, the only requirements —
wear something red, white or blue, show up
and march. *The Stars & Stripes Forever*
is followed by *Anchors Away*, but no one comes
for the music broadcast over W-I-L-I, boomboxes
lining the sidewalks and perched on the ledges
of windows so there's no need for uniforms
and brass bands. Church groups, clubs, proponents
of this-or-that, businesses, bureaus, kids on bikes
and skateboards, dogs, politicians and librarians
all convey themselves down Main Street, so
American you could cry, and of course you do
for the wonder of it, for the glory of the human pageant
and its gift for self-expression, and every possible
American is here, *grande y piqueño*, young and old,
rich, poor and middling. The Rainbow Coalition flares
its colors and The Wild Women of Willimantic
strut their stuff, as does The Precision Drill team
(marchers holding power drills), The Lawn Mowers'
Brigade, and The Baby Boomers' Unit (child and
stroller required). The Unitarians and The Boxing
Club march, antique car owners glide their gleaming
beauties, and this year six little girls dressed
as teacups for no special reason. The fluorescent
spiked-hair tattooed and leather-clad baldies show,
and various malcontents, but no cops — they're off
on the side streets directing traffic — for this parade
says fly the flag of your most outrageous disposition
and cry your barbaric yawp over the rooftops
of this old mill town. In this wild, discombobulated
American-style hubbub, we celebrate community
and "the blessing of liberty," we celebrate ourselves.

# Walt Whitman

Translated by Robert Bly

"But do you really want to see Whitman's house instead of Roosevelt's? I've never had this request before!"

The house is tiny and yellow, and next to the railroad track, like the hut of a switchman, in a small green patch of grass, marked out with whitewashed stones, beneath a single tree. Around it, the wide meadow area is open to the wind, which sweeps it, and us, and has polished the simple rough piece of marble which announces to the trains:

TO MARK THE BIRTHPLACE OF

WALT WHITMAN

THE GOOD GRAY POET

BORN MAY 31, 1819

ERECTED BY THE COLONIAL SOCIETY

OF HUNTINGTON IN 1905

Since the farmer doesn't seem to be at home, I walk around the house a couple of times, hoping to see something through the windowlets. Suddenly a man, tall, slow-moving and bearded, wearing a shirt and wide-brimmed hat — like the early photograph of Whitman — comes, from somewhere, and tells me, leaning on his iron bar, that he doesn't know who Whitman was, that he is Polish, that this house is his, and that he does not intend to show it to anyone. Then pulling himself up, he goes inside, through the little door that looks like a toy door.

Solitude and cold. A train goes by, into the wind. The sun, scarlet for an instant, dies behind the low woods, and in the swamp we walk past which is green and faintly blood-colored, innumerable toads are croaking in the enormous silence.

# Testament
# (Or, Homage to Walt Whitman)

*loveroot, silkthread, crotch and vine . . .*
— Walt Whitman

*I trust all joy.*
— Theodore Roethke

I, Erica Jong, in the midst of my life,
    having had two parents, two sisters,
    two husbands, two books of poems
    & three decades of pain,

        having cried for those who did not love me
        & those who loved me — but not enough
        & those whom I did not love —
        declare myself now for joy.

There is pain enough to nourish us everywhere;
    it is joy that is scarce.

There are corpses piled up to the mountains,
    & tears to drown in,
    & bile enough to swallow all day long.

Rage is a common weed.
Anger is cheap.

Righteous indignation
    is the religion of the dead
    in the house of the dead
    where the dead speak to each other
    in creaking voices,
    each arguing a more unhappy childhood
    than the other.

Unhappiness is cheap.
 Childhood is a universal affliction.
 I say to hell with the analysts of minus & plus,
 the life-shrinkers, the diminishers of joy.

I say to hell with anyone
 who would suck on misery
 like a pacifier
 in a toothless mouth.
 I say to hell with gloom.

Gloom is cheap.
 Every night the earth resolves for darkness
 & then breaks its resolve
 in the morning.

Every night the demon lovers
 come with their black penises like tongues,
 with their double faces,
 & their cheating mouths
 & their glum religions of doom.

Doom is cheap.
 If the apocalypse is coming,
 let us wait for it in joy.

Let us not gnash our teeth
 on the molars of corpses —
 though the molars of corpses
 are plentiful enough.

Let us not scorn laughter
 though scorn is plentiful enough.

Let us laugh & bring plenty to the scorners —
 for they scorn themselves.

I myself have been a scorner
    & have chosen scornful men,
      men to echo all that was narrow in myself,
      men to hurt me as I hurt myself.

In my stinginess,
    my friends have been stingy.
In my narrowness,
    my men have been mean.

I resolve now for joy.

If that resolve means I must live alone,
    I accept aloneness.

If the joy house I inhabit must be
    a house of my own making,
    I accept that making.

No doom-saying, death-dealing, fucker of cunts
    can undo me now.

No joy-denyer can deny me now.
    For what I have is undeniable.
    I inhabit my own house,
    the house of my joy.

"Unscrew the locks from the doors!
Unscrew the doors themselves from their jambs!"

Dear Walt Whitman,
    horny old nurse to pain,
    speaker of "passwords primeval,"
    merit-refuser, poet of body & soul —
    I scorned you at twenty
    but turn to you now

in the fourth decade of my life,
having grown straight enough
to praise your straightness,
& plain enough
to speak to you plain
& simple enough
to praise your simplicity.

The doors open.
The metaphors themselves swing open wide!

Papers fall from my desk,
     my desk teeters on the edge of the cosmos,
     & I commit each word to fire.

I burn!
All night I write in suns across the page.
I fuel the "body electric" with midnight oil.
I write in neon sperm across the air.

You were "hankering, gross, mystical, nude."
You astonished with the odor of your armpits.
You cocked your hat as you chose;
     you cocked your cock —
     but you knew "the Me myself."

You believed in your soul
     & believing, you made others
     believe in theirs.

The soul is contagious.
     One man catches another's
     like the plague;
     & we are all patient spiders
     to each other.

If we can spin the joythread
    & also catch it —

if we can be sufficient to ourselves,
    we need fear no entangling webs.

The loveroot will germinate.
The crotch will be a trellis for the vine,
    & our threads will all be intermingled silk.

How to spin joy out of an empty heart?
The joy-egg germinates even in despair.

Orgasms of gloom convulse the world;
    & the joy-seekers huddle together.

We meet on the pages of books & by beachwood fires.
We meet scrawled blackly in many-folded letters.
We know each other by free & generous hands.
We swing like spiders on each other's souls.

## Whitman Again

There is,
to rid of us morning,
a list of dues:
notes to follow,
books to think about before we write,
but think high,
of a yellow kite
above day
gathering wind to its sticks,
its hide tight,
bucking,
as if to slip
one long line
free of our hands.

# Kosmos

You shanghaied me to this oak,
Every blood-tipped leaf
Soliloquizing Billie's "Strange Fruit,"
Like that octoroon in New Orleans

Who showed you how passion
Ignited dogwoods, how it came
From inside the singing sap. You
Heard primordial notes of jazz

Murmuring up from the Mississippi,
A clink of chains in the green jurisdiction
Of ithyphallic totems, thinking your heart
Could run vistas with Crazy Horse

& runaway slaves. Sunset dock
To whorehouse, temple to hovel,
Your lines traversed America's
White space, driven by a train's syncopation.

2

Believing you could be everywhere
At once, you held the gatekeeper's daughter,
Lured by the hard eyes of his son,
On a voyage in your head

Like a face cut into Mount Rushmore.
You knew the curse was in the sperm
& egg, but had faith in the soil,
That it'd work itself out in generations,

How underground springs pierced bedrock.
How love pushed through jailhouse walls. Into the bedrooms of
presidents & horse thieves
Like oil sucked through machines in sweatshops

& factories. I followed you from my hometown
Where bedding an oak is bread on the table,
When your books, as if of flesh, were locked
In a glass case behind the check-out desk.


3

Wind-jostled foliage — a scherzo
Like a bellydancer adorned in bells.
A mulatto moon halved into yesterday
& tomorrow, a strange baluster

Full-bloomed. But you taught me home
Was wherever my feet took me,
Birdsong over stockyards or Orient.
Fused by handshake & blood,

Seed & testament, naked
Among fire-nudged thistle,
From the Rockies to below
Sea level, to the steamy bayous,

I traipsed your footpaths.
Falsehoods lay across the road,
Beside a watery swoon,
Stumbling blocks big as logs.

4

I'm back with the old folk who speak
In tongues, like your glossolalia
Of pure sense unfolding a hundred years.
Unlocked chemistry, we're tied to sex,
Spectral flower twisted out of the filigree
Of language, worked into a hope
Stubborn as crabgrass. You camped out,
Nude under god-hewn eyes.

Laughter in the trees behind a canebreak,
I know what song. Old hippie,
Before Selma & People's Park,
Your democratic nights were a vortex

Of waterlilies. The skin's cage
Opened by the mind. Everything
Flew apart, but came back like birds
To a tree after the blast of a shotgun.

# A Whitman Portrait

You know that portrait of him that caused such a ruckus?
The one where he's propped in that caneback chair
striking a pose so grave & heroic
you'd swear at first glance it was Odin or Lear or —
ah, but at that very moment you'll notice,
— as just about everyone finally does —
the butterfly perched on his right index finger.
& then you can see that Walt's sitting there
under that rakish sombrero & beard,
grandly amused, as much as to say:
*How splendid it is to see you my dear,*
*& what a propitious moment to call. . . .*
You can guess how his critics stewed over that one!
They'd fling up their arms in maniacal fury
& swear up & down that the thing was a fraud.
Why, it's nothing but papier mache! they would shriek.
A cardboard-&-wire photographer's prop!
Which slander, however absurd and transparent,
the populace simply assumed to be fact — till just
last September when high-resolution spectro-
analysis proved what any fool could have guessed:
she was just what she seemed: mortal & breathing.
A carbon-molecular creature like us. *Papilio*
*aristodemus*, now all but extinct.
The very swallowtail — golden-banded & blue-
tipped — that archeo-lepidopterists claim
could have been seen all over Camden that summer.
One of the millions scooting about thru the woods
& fields around Timber Creek Pond. Only, for
whatever odd reason, this one had taken a fancy to Walt.
When she wasn't flitting about in the fennel & parsley,

the neighbors would see her light on his wrist
or swing thru his beard or perch on his shoulder
like some sort of angel, or sprite, or familiar.
How he did it we don't know exactly,
but as the photographer set up his camera
Walt sat himself down by the open window
& hummed a few bars of Donizetti's *La Favorita*,
at which simple tune that bright little beauty
flitted in from the garden as if she'd been called to.
If it's true there exist fake butterflies
cut out of paper & wire, my guess is
they belong to a later generation of poets.
In any case, this one was made of the same stuff
as we are — felt pleasure & pain in abundance:
lit first on the broad brim of his hat, next at his
knee & at last on his finger. Was greeted by Walt
with a gruff, friendly laugh as one of his cronies —
at which very instant the chap with the camera
— who'd never dreamed he would see such a sight! —
triggered the shutter, preserving forever
that mischievous flight of felicitous whimsy.
This portrait at once majestic & tender,
& bathed in affection & grace & delight:
Walt Whitman & butterfly. Camden, New Jersey, 1883.

# A Civil War Veteran from Indiana Recalls Visiting with Walt Whitman in a Washington Hospital

Even now, as I stare into the fire,
I can see him sitting there, that
lonely old man whose eyes fluttered
like quail roosting beyond the snowy
white bush of his whiskers and hair.
At first when I came to at dusk
and saw him sitting there, through
my fever, I was suspicious. As you
can imagine! What could an old man
want in a ward of wounded and dying
soldiers that reeked of gangrene
and piss? But when he spoke,
I relaxed. I had never heard
such a voice. His words were salve
to my wound. He talked like one
of us, but somehow gentler.
He asked about my pain, if it was
better. I nodded. When I admitted
I was thirsty, he put water to my
lips. He wanted to know where my
folks lived, whether they'd heard
about my injury. When I shook
my head sideways and mumbled "Indiana,
southern Indiana," he said: "Oh, yes,
the hills. A Hoosier from the hills!"
He'd once sailed up the Ohio River
past Troy, he said, on his way back
from New Orleans. He wrote a letter
like I'd never read. It arrived like

balm for my mother's fears, beer
to my father's thirst for news. Mother
saved it till she died. "Don't worry,"
he wrote, "your brave son will be back
eating pawpaws soon." When I got back
enough strength to become a good listener,
he explained he'd gone all the way
from New York to Virginia looking
for his brother George; he'd been wounded
in the first Fredericksburg battle.
My God, how he loved to talk! Sometimes
I wondered who was the patient and who
was the aide. Outside the hospital
at Fredericksburg, he said, he found
"a heap of feet, arms, legs, and hands . . .
Enough to fill a whole horse cart!"
He shook his head, shuddered, and
sort of moaned: "And dead bodies
covered with brown woolen blankets."
He took a deep breath, then sighed:
"But George was alive and whole."
Sometimes when he looked into my eyes
from beyond that white bush, I thought
I might have once been his brother,
in some other world. I was by no means
the only soldier he visited. He'd come
into the ward coat and trouser pockets
bulging with gifts: apples, oranges,
sweet crackers, figs. Once he came
in carrying a jar of preserved raspberries
"donated by a lady." A few times I saw
him slip a coin into someone's moist
palm. Once I saw him lift a twist
of tobacco to an amputees's jaw.
Many's the time I watched him tear off
a sheet of paper from a pad, write
while he asked questions at the side

of the bed, and seal a letter into
an envelope. How that man loved
to write! To people from all over!
You'd have thought he was a parent himself.
He once confessed that he'd written many
a tender love letter for the wounded.
That made him chuckle. The night before
I left, he read to me from a book.
I had never heard anything like it.
It was like the person in that book
was talking right to me, had known
me all my life. He spoke my kind
of language. It was beautiful without
being fancy. It was natural as sun,
rain, and snow. The rhythm swelled
like the sea, as I imagined it to sound.
I could see leaves of grass growing
on the graves of soldiers. I could
see a young boy growing up on an island
with an Indian-sounding name. I could
feel the sun on my shoulders, hear
the surf splash on the shore. When his
voice ebbed like that tide, I looked
into his soft eyes, and told him how
good it was. He smiled, thanked me,
said he wrote the book himself.
Watching the fire fade, I can still
hear his salty voice roll like the sea.

# Dear Mr. Whitman,

*Vivas for those who have failed.*
— Walt Whitman

My husband,
and don't put the blame
there for if you had ever heard
about his life you would wonder
how
he has found out enough bad
luck
to call him a failure.
As in the case of the Plymouth.
A pleasant blue, decent rubber,
few dents, new door, but he
wouldn't know where
it came from first
thanks to his friends.
To make the point:
he did not apply for bad luck nor
did he ask for it.
What do I mean?
After class last night professor
said you —
may I say Walter? —
work as a nurse so you
would surely see things as
regards
to difficulties. Walter, you would
go far
to find a man to go bust as
much as Mike.

As for the vivas, Thanks
but nevermind, Mike said.
Nevermind and forget it, he said
for he has other feelings that
vivas
are of little or no help.

  I tried,

  Trudy

# I Sing the Body Electric

People sit numbly at the counter
waiting for breakfast or service.
Today it's Hartford, Connecticut
more than twenty-five years after
the last death of Wallace Stevens.
I have come in out of the cold
and wind of a Sunday morning
of early March, and I seem to be
crying, but I'm only freezing
and unpeeled. The waitress brings
me hot tea in a cracked cup,
and soon it's all over my paper,
and so she refills it. I read
slowly in *The New York Times*
that poems are dying in Iowa,
Missoula, on the outskirts of Reno,
in the shopping galleries of Houston.
We should all go to the grave
of the unknown poet while the rain
streaks our notebooks or stand
for hours in the freezing winds
off the lost books of our fathers
or at least until we can no longer
hold our pencils. Men keep coming
in and going out, and two of them
recall the great dirty fights
between Willy Pep and Sandy Sadler,
between little white perfection
and death in red plaid trunks.
I want to tell them I saw
the last fight, I rode out

to Yankee Stadium with two deserters
from the French Army of Indochina
and back with a drunken priest
and both ways the whole train
smelled of piss and vomit, but no
one would believe me. Those are
the true legends better left to die.
In my black rain coat I go back
out into the gray morning and dare
the cars on North Indemnity Boulevard
to hit me, but no one wants trouble
at this hour. I have crossed
a continent to bring these citizens
the poems of the snowy mountains,
of the forges of hopelessness,
of the survivors of wars they
never heard of and won't believe.
Nothing is alive in this tunnel
of winds of the end of winter
except the last raging of winter,
the cats peering smugly from the homes
of strangers, and the great stunned sky
slowly settling like a dark cloud
lined only with smaller dark clouds.

# Whitman

*I say we had best look our times and lands searchingly in the face, like a physician diagnosing some deep disease.*
— Democratic Vistas

*. . . look for me under your boot-soles.*


On Long Island, they moved my clapboard house
Across a turnpike, then
Named a shopping center after me!

Now that I'm required reading in your high schools,
Teen-agers call me a fool.
Now what I sang
Stops breathing, like the daughter too high on drugs
To come back, in your arms. Her white dress
So hopeful, & beside the point.
And yet

It was only when no one could believe in me
That I began living again —
In the thin whine of Montana fence wire,
In the transparent, cast off garments hung
In the windows of the poorest families,
In the glad music of Charlie Parker.
At times now,
I even come back to watch you
From the eyes of a taciturn boy at Malibu.
Across the counter at the beach concession stand,
I sell you hot dogs, Pepsis, cigarettes —
My blond hair long, greasy, & swept back
In a vain old ducktail, deliciously
Out of style.
And no one notices.

Once, I even came back as myself,
An aging homosexual who ran a Tilt-a-Whirl
At country fairs, a Mardi Gras tattoo on my left shoulder;
And the chilled paint on each gondola
Changing color as it picked up speed, made me smile.
I thought you caught the meaning of my stare:
Still water, merciless
As my laughter.

A Cosmos. One of the roughs.

And Charlie Parker's grave in Kansas City
Covered with weeds.

Leave me alone.
A father who's outlived his only child.

To find me now will cost you everything.

# Ode to Walt Whitman

*Translated by Betty Jean Craige*

Along the East River and the Bronx,
the young men were singing showing their waists,
with the wheel, the oil, the leather and the hammer.
Ninety thousand miners were taking silver out of the rocks
and the boys were drawing ladders and perspectives.

But nobody was sleeping,
nobody wanted to be the river,
nobody loved the large leaves,
nobody loved the blue tongue of the beach.

Along the East River and Queensborough
the young men were fighting with industry,
and the jews were selling to the faun of the river
the rose of the circumcision
and the sky emptied over the bridges and the roofs
herds of bison pushed by the wind.

But nobody was stopping,
nobody wanted to be a cloud,
nobody was seeking the ferns
or the yellow wheel of the drum

When the moon comes out
the pulleys will turn to disturb the sky;
a border of needles will enclose the memory
and the coffins will carry off those who do not work.

New York of mud,
New York of wire and death.
What angel do you carry hidden in your cheek?
What perfect voice will speak the truths of the wheat?
Who will speak the terrible dream of the stained anemones?

Not a single moment, old beautiful Walt Whitman,
have I stopped seeing your beard full of butterflies,
or your shoulders of corduroy wasted by the moon,
or your muscles of a virginal Apollo,
or your voice like a column of ash;
old man beautiful as the cloud
who cried like a bird
with his sex pierced by a needle,
enemy of the satyr,
enemy of the vine
and lover of bodies under the heavy cloth.
Not a single moment, virile beauty
who on mountains of carbon, advertisements and railroads,
dreamed of being a river and sleeping as a river
with that comrade who would put in your breast
a small pain of an unknowing leopard.

Not a single moment, Adam of blood, male,
lone man in the sea, old beautiful Walt Whitman,
for the rooftops,
clustered in the bars,
leaving in bunches from the sewers
trembling between the legs of the chauffeurs
or turning around on platforms of wormwood,
the perverts, Walt Whitman, dreamed of you.

Also that! As well! And they fling themselves
upon your luminous and chaste beard,
blonds from the north, blacks from the sand,
crowds of shouts and gestures,

like cats and like serpents,
the perverts, Walt Whitman, the perverts
turbid with tears, flesh for the whiplash,
boot or bite of the animal trainers.

Also that! As well! Stained fingers
point to the bank of your dream
when the friend eats your apple
with a light taste of gasoline
and the sun sings through the navels
of the young men who play beneath the bridges.

But you were not seeking scratched eyes,
or the dark bog where they submerge the boys,
or the frozen saliva,
or the curves wounded like a toad's belly
that the perverts carry in cars and on terraces
while the moon lashes them on the corners of terror.

You were seeking a nude who might be like a river,
bull and dream that might unite the wheel and the seaweed,
father of your agony, camelia of your death,
who would cry in the flames of your hidden equator.

For it is just that man not seek his pleasure
in the jungle of blood of the following morning.
The sky has beaches for the evasion of life
and there are bodies that should not be repeated at dawn.

Agony, agony, dream, ferment and dream.
This is the world, friend, agony, agony.
The dead decompose beneath the clock of the cities,
the war passes crying with a million gray rats,
the rich give to their mistresses
small lighted dying ones,
and life is not noble, or good, or sacred.

Man can, if he wants, conduct his desire
through the coral vein or celestial nude.
Tomorrow the loves will be rocks and Time
a breeze that comes sleeping through the branches.

Therefore I do not raise my voice, old Walt Whitman,
against the boy who writes
the name of a girl on his pillow,
nor against the youth who dresses as a bride
in the darkness of the closet,
nor against the lonely men of the casinos
who drink with nausea the water of prostitution,
nor against the men with the green gaze
who love men and burn their lips in silence.

But I do raise my voice against you, perverts of the cities,
of swelling flesh and filthy thought,
mothers of mud, harpies, sleepless enemies
of the Love that distributes wreaths of joy.

Against you always, who give to the young men
drops of filthy death with bitter venom.
Against you always,
*Faeries* of North America,
*Pájaros* of Havana,
*Jotos* of Mexico,
*Sarasas* of Cadiz,
*Apios* of Seville,
*Cancos* of Madrid,
*Floras* of Alicante,
*Adelaidas* of Portugal.

Perverts everywhere, assassins of doves!
Slaves of the woman, bitches of their boudoirs,
open in the plazas with fan fever
or ambushed in motionless landscapes of hemlock.

May there be no district! Death
flows from your eyes
and groups gray flowers on the bank of the mud.
May there be no district! Watch out!
That the confused, the pure,
the classic, the distinguished, the entreating ones
may shut the doors of the bacchanal.

And you, handsome Walt Whitman, sleep on the rivers of the Hudson
with your beard towards the pole and your hands open.
Soft clay or snow, your tongue is calling
comrades to watch your disembodied gazelle.
Sleep, nothing remains.

A dance of walls shakes the meadows
and America is flooded in machines and sobs.
I want the strong air of the deepest night
to take away flowers and letters from the arch where you sleep
and a black child to announce to the whites of the gold
the coming of the reign of the wheat.

# Walt Whitman's Brain Dropped on Laboratory Floor

At his request, after death, his brain was removed
for science, phrenology, to study, and
as the mortuary assistant carried it (I suppose
in a jar but I hope cupped
in his hands) across the lab's stone floor, he dropped it.

You could ask a forensic pathologist
what that might look like. He willed his brain,
as I said, for study — its bumps and grooves,
analyzed, allowing a deeper grasp
of human nature, potential (so phrenology believed),
and this kind of intense look, as opposed to mere fingering

of the skull's outer ridges, valleys, would afford
particular insight. So Walt believed.
He had already scored high (between a 6 and a 7) for Ego.
And as if we couldn't guess from his verses, he scored
high again (a 6 and a 7 — 7 the highest possible!)

in Amativeness (sexual love) and Adhesiveness
(friendship, brotherly love) when before his death
his head was read. He earned only a 5 for Poetic Faculties,
but that 5, pulled and pushed by his other numbers,
allowed our father of poesy to lay down some words
in the proper order on the page. That our nation

does not care does not matter, much.
That his modest federal job was taken from him,
and thus his pension, does not matter at all.
And that his brain was dropped and shattered, a cosmos,
on the floor, matters even less.

## A Whit for Whitman

So large, so over-the-top, so willing to expand and even in grief exalt,
You're good and gray, and I, much smaller, made this couplet for you, Walt.

# Hopkins and Whitman

Hard to imagine two men more unlike, the one
a solitary wrestling in his cell with palpable Doubt,
the other striding the continent in great unbooted
certainty. And yet there was that kinship, pitched

past pitch of grief, and battlefield nursing —
"What is removed drops horribly in a pail" —
and Hopkins's own admission: "I know Walt Whitman's
mind to be more like my own than any man's living.

As he is a very great scoundrel, this is not
a pleasant confession." How magnetic the expanse
between fastidious and crude when cast
into the field of dappled things! For Hopkins,

the cows and finches and trout of a world whose
stippled shadows served to throw into relief
the Godlight, though his own scree of darkness —
the mountainslide, the mind's cliffs of fall —

was for days heaped on days impenetrable;
for Whitman, the skewed patchwork of criminal
and child twinned in one body and one land,
sending out its pied beauty in a cruel Morse —

blue/gray, blue/gray — horrible and redemptive
at once, for the Godlight shone through the stippled
bandages . . . This was a man and country
straining to heal itself, something the English

priest in exile's Dublin knew something
about. Cold Ireland must have warmed a little
when the Classics Professor, Society of Jesus,
opened the newspaper to rawly dazzling American

nakedness. Unruly America would have bent
at once to the rigors of principle, had those
rigors been in print. But it was less their lives
which rang accord than it was their deaths,

though Whitman had his pharaonic tomb,
secured with locks against robbers, and Hopkins
a bare-stripped room. It was their deaths
that knelled through their poems from the earliest

verses: Whitman, so much a part
of the sea he loved and feared, drowned
in the oceanic emphysema of his lungs. His last
day he was moved onto a sort of water bed

on the floor, "Oh I feel so good" his last
words when he heard the waves falling against
his sides. And Hopkins, spent with the typhoid
his fevered poems had long pointed to,

after great agitation, this clearing: "I am so happy."
And surely God stood at his pillow then.
And surely the sea made its smooth reclamation.
If we take heart in anything, it is a serene death

and the poems unfolding in reverse that we might
see death in all its guises, back to the first
awareness: "We hear our hearts grate on themselves;
it kills to bruise them dearer."

# Second-Born Son
## Lines for Walt Whitman Composed on Nantucket Island

I.

This house, September, and a woman
even you could believe in. I came here
on a ferry to write these lines about you, I
in my thirty-sixth year in perfect health,
as you would say, as you did say, and I too
a second-born son enamored of ferries:
the continuous white froth behind, the sea-birds
gliding impossibly close to water or diving
for scraps as you did into your chaos,
content with what scraps you could find there.
Sideswiped by any grace, how the faces
of strangers undid you, Tuesday through Monday —
cab drivers, ferrymen, widows — that world
you owned like a lamp you could not stop
rubbing. But especially on ferries,
wide-mouthed and handsome: who worried
about destinations? And the sun and moon
on opposite horizons falling and rising
as though connected by wires, the sun orange
and the moon orange. And you between sea floor
and sky floor, your reflection pendant, a creature
alike of air as of water, the face that you loved
there wistful and whiskered and your hat cocked
as you pleased, and your slow omnivorous smile.

2.

The light here could take you like touch
away. Goldenrod. Bird Flash. Shadow.
But this wind — howl-sick, unsettling — listen:
whistle in the underpinnings, window-caresser.
Houses you built with your brothers in Brooklyn,
a trade learned from your father who, even as you
whistled down your reckonings toward tomorrow,
lay there dying of what he missed, some lack
you tried hard to supply with your words —
supple, insinuating, carefree, careening toward
disasters you had not begun, luckily, to understand.
Between the soles of your feet and that hard
earth what a sad distance. Earth and father
you coupled, saving for mothers the sea,
or the moon — sagging, yellow-breasted, brown-
nippled — oh how you courted it, eclipsing
with your father's house-building hands
its uncentering brilliance at the last minute.
Hammerblow and firedamp. So far down
no wind would howl there but only the dark
interstices of your firstlove floating you back
to such omnipotence as you could muster.
All your moons are mothers, and the womb,
given its own good time, has its own revenge.


3.

Which self was it, Walt, that called you
to the window that dusk as your father
lay dying, your only older brother going mad,
your youngest brother crippled and half-witted,
your mother knitting her yarn of helplessness
around you all tighter and tighter — to that window
where you saw prefigured in clouds off Long Island

your own face and heard the late mockingbird
speak your name in the elms? I see you there
tentative as the first stars, turning not bright
but transparent as glass through which you wander
into the evening to become the lover of lonely
housewives, the begetter of invisible children,
sounder of depths, food for the hungry
who do not know they are hungry, salt
for their food and their wounds, flesh-fiber
and muscle-fiber, mica on the rock, dust mote
in the day-ending light that streams past your body
and shapes on the silent form of your father
the elongated shadow of his second-born,
looming like nightfall. And in the manuscript
the long dusty avenues of your lines rise
weightlessly from the page and wind off toward
some zero of expectation, high over Paumanok.

# To Walt Whitman on America's Birthday

Walt Whitman has just walked into the room,
and for a moment,
though everyone is looking at him,
no one goes forward to greet him.

It is Walt Whitman, after all,
and what could we possibly say to him
or he to us
that we wouldn't find embarrassing in the morning.

Luckily, someone rescues us from the silence,
someone I know vaguely,
was introduced to once at a function much like this one,
have said hello to in the elevator once or twice
but who works in another department
and so will become someone I greet
less and less over the years
until I do not recognize him at all
and he returns to being someone
I never met.

This person, this someone,
whose name even now escapes me,
asks Mr. Whitman if he would like a glass of sherry.
It is that kind of function.
A waiter in a white coat
who is also a graduate student in economics
appears with a glass of sherry.
Walt Whitman is too stunned to say thank you.
He drinks instead,
looking into the glass.

The person, the same person,
asks several questions.
He wishes to put everyone at ease.
Walt Whitman is already at ease.

He does not hear the questions.
He drinks his sherry, rather quickly,
puts the empty glass in his coat pocket
and leaves.

When he is safely gone,
we all have a good laugh
at that one.

# Reaching Around

For Walt Whitman

*I have perceiv'd that to be with those I like is enough . . .*
*To pass among them or touch any one, or rest my arm ever so*
*        lightly round his or her neck for a moment, what is this then?*
*I do not ask any more delight, I swim in it as in a sea.*

1972  We're all uproarious, Philip and I and his
        preposterously pregnant wife who can't get up,
        their sofa's sagged too low, just since yesterday
        she's too immense — or tired, it's late,
        I should think about rising, but for me as well
        that's hard. Harder each time in fact
        to leave this house, though on the carpet I'm
        dissembling more and more: for the past hour
        I've been aware, as mercifully they're not
        yet, of the slow ache secretly uncoiling
        down the long inner muscles of my arms,
        clamped round me for safe-keeping. I can visualize
        these muscles, as in a Ben-Gay ad,
        spangled to show the pain. The pain bears lengthwise
        down, bears down, bears down; my elephantine
        friend, hilarity-weakened, tries again to heave
        herself out of her seat, it's her they want
        mostly, she's great, who wouldn't? Shhh don't don't

        Driving home I sober up at once.
        The outlook's awful, instinct says not a prayer.
        At arm's length sure, they like me, I can feel it,
        but the least whiff of serious weirdness — oh,
        *damn* the damn thing! clumsily complicating
        what should be unaffected, plain . . . poor arms,
        they want to reach around, that's all, an impulse

so natural it's cruel to have to inhibit,
so mulish it's exhausting to, and so
imperative it's freakish. Don't I know.

1955   Scout camp at twelve. Through sunburned weedfields
my group of girls kicks tentward. Grasshoppers
explode about us, our shirts and shorts, and limbs,
accumulate those smaller leaf-green hopping
things that live in tall weeds in Ohio.
A prickly walk, I like it, glad to be
one among them at this ugliest age
of inch-thick glasses, nose and sailor hat
and mammoth chest, and so forth. So I've got
my copious third period now — so what!
To my mind I'm no Girl, I'm just plain Scout.

We're telling what we're going to be; I volunteer
"A missionary to Africa." Touched by this,
our nicest counselor, Margie, slides a half-hug
round my stiff shoulder. For me to shrug
from under growling "Mush!" is automatic,
I really have to, yet in a trice I'm dying
to take back both: her arm, my churlish gesture —
unthinkable. We both feel bad.
I scuff on, blazing trail through prickly heat,
Queen Anne's lace, bugs on springs, all trussed up tight
in a self-image, Billy Goat Gruff's own Kid.

1968   A stone-cold toad-hideous
gargoyle squats on a sofa  croaking  croaking
warts all blood . . .
aghast, my friends strip beds,
pile covers on, but nothing warms
or comforts, or shuts me up: *Be physical*
*with kids*, obsessively. The parents
behold my state in wonderment, confer in whispers;
their little boy, who's two,

runs in circles endlessly,
hollering till nerve-ends
squirm gibbering through lumpy skin, while I
don't stop and don't stop
hoarsely warning his macho dad: hold him, cuddle him.
Often as I've since been thanked
for this advice, or order, I still marvel
it was heeded. "You
kidding? The envoy from the brink of doom? My God,
that shaking voice, those cold thin fingers
clutching every blanket in the house
around you — you had authority,
believe me, I *believed* you."

1963   Classic Hall, mid-evening and mid-May.
I'm nominally reading in "my" office
but concentration's poor. Far down along
the dark corridor, light squares through a doorframe —
my teacher-mentor-"father," working late.
How soon can I go calling? Wait.
Don't crowd. Studying him closer than Shakespeare,
his ease, warmth, gentleness, his . . . anti-Gruffness,
I've glimpsed some happier ways to be not spineless
than Dad's. A mild and passive missionary
he thinks I *go at* things too hard. (He would.)
Well, fine — I'll be his auto-convert

                                    Light
snaps out, spatter of rubber footsteps — *wait!*
Slam book, grab notes and pen, pelt headlong down
the black stairs, catch him up too breathless — Hi!
I just this minute finished *Henry the Fifth!*
Isn't that last act awful? Courtly love —
Katharine — "God of battles" — Falstaff/Hal —
The door; revealing racket muted against
a close, soft, honeysuckle-hyperbolic
Hoosier spring night. Between two breaths I'm offered

a lift back to the dorm. "Sure, thanks a lot!"
On flows and flows the babbling brook of language,
undammable    we're halfway to the car
his sudden warm enclosing hand    his voice
a chuckle    mine a plug-jerked radio

1979 Whitman, when I read over what you wrote
I have to wonder. Takes one to know one, right?
You doted on yourself, there was that lot of you
and all so luscious; you found no sweeter fat
than stuck to your own bones. Oh yeah?
No doubts then? It's our weakness to confuse
wish and conviction, ought-to-be with is,
and something in your voice . . . but if I'm wrong
and you're not bluffing, Walt, how happy you were
in that belief. I'm mired, I'm pretty sure,
in doubt for keeps. It creeps and creeps along,
a glacial progress I extrapolate
will have me hugging friends, age 68,
in 2010; I don't call that a cure.

The touch that heals? The laying on of hands?

When (in 1970) on the Delaware
I was the Scout camp counselor,
not for the first time nor the last, we had
this problem child. Obnoxious fat complainer,
she hated camp, crafts, swimming, cookouts, hikes —
Ready to brain the brat, I overheard
Margaret, my assistant, remark offhand
as if to state the obvious, "That kid
just needs to be held and held." Dumb stare: she did?
I of all people had the least excuse
not to sense that. The change in the little wretch
amazed us all. And hugging her felt *good*,
how can I put this right? almost as though

that thistly girl were me at her age, ten —
as though my reflex fendings-off had been
taken for what they were, and been ignored.

Balky, sulky, stiff in my arms as wood,
what was her name? She'd be in college now,
that camper who alone could tell us what
came of our cuddling — anything? If not
enduringly for her, to me it's meant
ever since then — that no child's need
gnarl into mine unmet — I've been released
to reach toward children every way one can,
help them be certain, clear to the marrow-lattice,
the fat that sticks to their bones is sweeter than sweet,
self-evident as weight and sight, so they
may never in their lives endure self-loathing
or self-constraint because of "a few light kisses,
a few embraces, a reaching around of arms"
that didn't happen. Otherwise no — except
as, clustered in a beaten space between
peaked huts, Kikuyu watch a white fanatic's
kind, sweaty, earnest face, or classroomful
of undergraduates sits forward rapt —

for who's the missionary *alias*
professor now, who strains to touch and change
minds with a mind? (I never saw this, strange —
language as sublimated touch, ideas
as sublimated — something . . .) Yet despite
that half-truth, and how stirring it can be
to touch a book and seem to touch a man,
flesh that embraces flesh still satisfies
our childish fat-and-bones' avidity
better than "Crossing Brooklyn Ferry" can
— though he was right.

*Envoi*

Whoever I am holding you now in hand
Has understood how much that luscious lot
You rightly said you were would understand
This long hug made of words that say I'm not.

# Postcard to Walt Whitman from Siena

Today the windy Italian air was clean as the air of Montauk,
I walked through a huge vaulted hall,
a Renaissance hospital opposite the Duomo,
and I thought of you, Walt Whitman, in your forties,
writing letters for the wounded and dying —
to nurse the horribly wounded,
you did not need to think of them as Jesus.
In the dark galleries, a kind of gossip
about the life of Christ,
the paintings are "gold ground,"
gold leaf, not leaves of grass. The painters
worked for the honor of illumination,
did not sign their work that was a form of prayer —
a signature can deflower a lily.
I saw a cradle that was a cathedral rocking,
I remembered you sang Italian arias
and the Star-Spangled Banner in your bathtub.
At five o'clock I heard the rosary,
the *joys* and *sorrows* of the Virgin,
had a café latte, then returned to hear the litany:
*star of the sea, lily of the valley, tower of ivory* —
something like you praising America.

# Reading "Crossing Brooklyn Ferry"
# on a Summer Morning

In the quiet of the barn loft study I've read the poem again —
and the breeze comes through the screen of the big window and lifts
    the old lace tablecloth hung for a curtain and blows a
    coolness into my face.
Birds are rustling under the eave near my head, beyond the gray
    beam with its delicate cracks of dryness.
The veins in the back of my hand make ridges in the skin —
and a spider web trembles from a rafter.
It is another clear morning.
A shaggy man is sitting alone late at night scratching at a sheet of paper,
and like the marks carved twenty thousand years ago on an antler
    in a cave, which say "someone was alive here,"
these scratchings are secret messages told to everyone.
"The dark threw its patches down upon me also. . . ."
He listens to the night, and remembers the flow of the river,
    and the men and women on the deck, and the curious crown of
    beams of light his shadow wore on the water,
and feels the pull of his words in his chest, and his hand scuffs
    slowly across the page.

# A Modern Poet

Crossing at rush hour the Walt Whitman Bridge,
He stopped at the Walt Whitman Shopping Center
And bought a paperback copy of *Leaves of Grass*.
Fame is the spur, he figured; given a Ford
Foundation Fellowship, he'd buy a Ford.

# Ode to Walt Whitman

*Translated by Willis Barnstone*

I don't remember
at what age
or where,
whether in the great wet South
or on the terrifying
coast, under the quick
screech of sea gulls,
I touched a hand and it was
the hand of Walt Whitman:
I strolled the earth
with naked feet,
I walked on the pasture,
over the firm dew
of Walt Whitman.

During
my youth
that hand
went with me in everything,
its dew,
its patriarchal pine firmness, its extension of meadows,
and its mission of circulatory peace.

Without
scorning
the earth's
gifts,
the copious
curve of the spire
or the initial

purple
of wisdom,
you
taught me
to be American,
raised
my eyes
to books,
toward
the treasure
of the buckwheat and oats:
broad
in the transparency
of the fields,
you made me see
the lofty
tutelary
mountain. Out of the subterranean
echo,
you rescued everything
for me,
everything,
everything born
you harvested
galloping in the alfalfa,
cutting me poppies,
visiting
rivers,
showing up in the evening
at the kitchens.

But your spade
dug up not only
earth
into light:
you unearthed

a man
and the slave
humiliated
with you, balancing
the black dignity of his stature
his cheerfulness
as he walked on
conquering.

To the stoker
below
in the boiler room,
you sent
a delicate basket
of strawberries,
at every corner of your people
your verse
came for a visit
and was a hunk
of clean body,
your poems showed up
like
your own fisherman's beard
or the grave road of your acacia legs.

Among the soldiers came
your silhouette
of the bard, the nurse,
the nocturnal healer
who knows
the sound
of breathing during death pangs
and waits with dawn
for the silent
return
of life

Good baker!
Older brother cousin
of my roots,
cupola
of the araucaria pine,
it's
already
a hundred
years
that wind
passes over your pasture herbs
and its germinations
without wearing out your eyes.

New
and cruel years in your nation:
persecutions, tears,
jails,
poisoned weapons
and enraged wars
haven't crushed
the grass of your book,
the vital spring water
of your freshness.
And, ay!
those
who assassinated Lincoln
now
lie in his bed,
they demolished
his presidential chair
of fragrant wood
and
erected a throne
splattered with calamity
and blood.

But
your voice
sings in
suburban
stations,
in
the
evening
landing docks,
your word
like dark water,
your people
white
and black,
the poor
people,
plain people
like all
peoples,
do not forget
your bell:
they gather singing
under
the magnitude
of your spacious life:
among the peoples your love strolls
caressing
the plain growth
of fellowship across the earth.

# Nurse Whitman

You move between the soldiers' cots
the way I move among my dead,
their white bodies laid out in lines.

You bathe the forehead, you bathe the lip, the cock,
as I touch my father, as if the language
were a form of life.

You write their letters home, I take the dictation
of his firm dream lips, this boy
I love as you love your boys.

They die and you still feel them. Time
becomes unpertinent to love,
to the male bodies in beds.

We bend over them, Walt, taking their breath
soft on our faces, wiping their domed brows,
stroking back the coal-black Union hair.

We lean down, our pointed breasts
heavy as plummets with fresh spermy milk —
we conceive, Walt, with the men we love, thus, now,
we bring to fruit.

# With Whitman at the Friendship Hotel

I call out crazed in fever in a room
in Peking where I've come afraid and alone
to find, something, the words maybe.
My family looks out from the gulf behind
their photographs on the rickety desk.

So I stand. With a bottle of red wine
and no talk for days, no talk
from my neighbors puzzled and rushed,
the Chinese frozen in awe untouching,
and here, in the chest of all that is lost,
I read, out loud, Walt Whitman.

Someone's voice cracks, gathers, grows
calm by my feet on the green wash of rug,
and waves this meeting aside. Brother,
brother, here is our home. Who knows
what powers the world! I love the man.

# Reading with the Poets

Whitman among the wounded, at the bedside,
kissing the blood off boys' faces, sometimes stilled
faces, writing their letters, writing the letters
home, saying, sometimes, the white prayers, helping,
sometimes, with the bodies or holding the bodies
down. The boy with the scar that cuts through his speech,
who's followed us here to the Elizabeth
Zane Memorial and Cemetery, wants
to speak nevertheless on the Civil War's
stone-scarred rows of dead and the battle here
just outside of Wheeling equal in death to
Gettysburg because no doctor between the war
and Pittsburgh was possible. Boys dressed like men

and men would gangrene first before the shock of
the saw and scalpel. Three days between this part
of the Ohio River and Pittsburgh. He
knows, he is here since then a child of history
and knows Elizabeth Zane saved all she could.
Keats all his wounded life wanted to be a healer,
which he was, once at his mother's bedside, failed,
once at his brother's, failed. Whitman in Washington
failed: how many nights on the watch and it broke
him, all those broken boys, all those bodies blessed
into the abyss. Now the poem for Lincoln,
now the boy with the scar almost singing, now
the oldest surviving poet of the war
reading one good line, then another, then
the song of the hermit thrush from the ground cover.
Lincoln's long black brooding body sailed in a train,
a train at the speed of the wind blossoming,

filling and unfilling the trees, a man's slow
running. Whitman had nowhere to go, so I
leave thee lilac with heart-shaped leaves, he says at
last, and went to the other side with the corpses,
myriads of them, soldiers' white skeletons,
far enough into the heart of the flower
that none of them suffered, none of them grieved, though
the living had built whole cities around them.

Keats at his medical lectures drew flowers.
Not from indifference, not from his elegance:
his interest couldn't bear the remarkable
screams of the demonstrations. He sat there, still
a boy, already broken, looking into the living
body, listening to the arias of the spirit
climbing. So the boy at the graves of the Union
singing, saying his vision, seeing the bodies
broken into the ground. Now the poem for Lincoln.
Now the oldest surviving poet still alive
weaving with the audience that gossamer,
that thread of the thing we find in the voice again.
Now in the night our faces kissed by the healer.

# A Pact

I make a pact with you, Walt Whitman —
I have detested you long enough.
I come to you as a grown child
Who has had a pig-headed father;
I am old enough now to make friends.
It was you that broke the new wood,
Now is a time for carving.
We have one sap and one root —
Let there be commerce between us.

# Walt Whitman

The master-songs are ended, and the man
That sang them is a name. And so is God
A name; and so is love, and life, and death,
And everything. But we, who are too blind
To read what we have written, or what faith
Has written for us, do not understand:
We only blink and wonder.

Last night it was the song that was the man,
But now it is the man that is the song.
We do not hear him very much to-day:
His piercing and eternal cadence rings
Too pure for us — too powerfully pure,
Too lovingly triumphant, and too large;
But there are some that hear him, and they know
That he shall sing to-morrow for all men,
And that all time shall listen.

The master-songs are ended? Rather say
No songs are ended that are ever sung,
And that no names are dead names. When we write
Men's letters on proud marble or on sand,
We write them there forever.

## A Porter on the Trail

In 1966,
when I started down the trail,
I carried a copy of
*The Poems of Walt Whitman*
in my rucksack.

I am not a learned man,
and I know only
two poems by heart:
"Kim Van Kieu"[1]
and "Song of Myself."

I would read as I walked
from North to South, and back.
I could share "Kieu" with anyone,
but had less opportunity to discuss "Song"
with my comrades.

Still, I drew strength from Whitman's poetry,
and optimism too. He wrote,
"All goes onward and outward . . ." and
"To die is different from what anyone supposed,
and luckier."

I wondered
how a nation
that gave birth to Walt Whitman
could also produce
napalm and Agent Orange.

1. "Kim Van Kieu" — the classic Vietnamese epic poem of selflessness.

He wrote,
"This is the grass that grows
wherever the land is and the water is,
This is the common air
that bathes the globe."

One day, near Khe Sanh, we captured a GI.
I was excited, and asked him about
"Song of Myself."
But the American said
he'd never heard of Walt Whitman.

# Against Whitman

Too many speak of whip-poor-wills
as if they knew them.
The trout is not my friend.
Oh, I hear a whistling in the trees.
I hear them praying in their tents,
Sunday afternoons. God's creatures:
I don't even know their nesting place.
I suppose I've been a growling dog,
a dusk, a thunderstorm, an ant
creeping up a leg. Spit, testes,
pine sap, sewage, kisses, maple leaf.
God's sopranos, the whip-poor-wills,
sing for hours at a time.
Do you suppose they mate for life?
I hardly know when I'm inside you.
Don't hate the stranger in me.
I also wish the wall of skin
were just another bridge to cross.

# Reading Whitman's *Democratic Vistas*

in a Burger King kills
    time, what my fourteen-year-old
        asks of me as she skips

up two studio steps to get an hour's
    worth of arpeggio runs & one-
        half share in the practice duets

for the flute. I sit alone
    in the corner booth, playing
        my breath, pianissimo, on the wing-

like steam rising from the styrofoam cup
    of coffee before me. Outside, all
        blackness & rain gutters

beneath brooding, Angus-colored thunderheads
    that restlessly stampede our way.
        And yet, inside, nothing stirs, not

the artificial ivy nor even the piped-in
    Muzak with a penchant for strings
        in a middling range. Here,

the only longing's for another passionless
    refill of coffee. Walt, I wonder
        what's become of "the great poems of death"

you dreamt of for the twentieth century.
    See, even those exorbitant storms,
        the cats & dogs of our youth,

aren't any longer. In the parking lot
　　this half-hearted spring rain has begun
　　　　to pelt the pavement & the marigolds in

cement pots as three joggers windsprint
　　around the corner & inside under cover.
　　　　Amazingly, they jog on in place

until the rains pass, like wind-up toys
　　in aerobic time to an inner tempo,
　　　　their day-glo jackets skin-wet & luminous

beneath the incessant tubes of fluorescent
　　lighting. Now, out of the blue,
　　　　I spot Pamela, ducking from awning

to awning through the fizzling drizzle,
　　her sheet music & flute tucked under one arm,
　　　　her metronome swinging

at the end of the other.

# Whitman Stock-Taking, Cataloguing

*Stock-taking, inventory, is the first effort of the mind to make itself at home . . . We see it in the*
*Homeric catalogue and poetic inventory of Whitman. But how does one do it where the home will*
*not stay put? Where the stock of items on the shelves changes every day?*
— Wright Morris, *The Territory Ahead*

Me *imperturbe*, standing, imperturbable, surveying the big country in rough-hewn,
    limping language, seeking the barbaric yawp;

*Allons*, rushing ahead in pseudo-language, fighting out of immigration's Tower
    of Babel to a new American tone, stock-taking, inventory, a bursting catalogue
    of vision;

*Ya-Honk*, the wild gander leading his flock through the Big Sky back to the frontier
    dream where Indians wait with grave faces contemplating the meaning of
    Reservations, lost land as enigmatic, agonizing camp-metaphors;

*Pent-up, aching rivers* driving pent-up, aching language down the Mississippi to
    New Orleans, following the terrible currents of slavery, "a woman's body at
    auction . . . the teeming mother of mothers," slavery as the incestuous
    relationship, the grotesque purchase of sexual mothers;

*A woman waits for me*, "They know how to swim, row, ride, wrestle, shoot, run,
    strike, retreat, advance, resist, defend themselves," they know everything,
    these Amazons, new society of aggressive force, women warriors on the
    frontier, schoolteacher, nun, whore, wife, impossible future fantasies hiding
    slaves and masters, haunted homosexuals becoming isolated singers;

*The demand for facts*, an endless naming of objects and persons, "but woe to the age
    or land in which these things, movements, stopping at themselves, do not tend
    to ideas," ideas vanishing in Civil War, nursing wounded comrades, O
    Camerado, a great feminine nurse bending over desperate spiritual and
    physical wounds, washing off the blood of insanity, feeling the uncanny "body
    electric," flesh as leaves of grass;

*The long line gathering*, flowing out into space in a curious procession, low-hanging
    moons, solitary guests from Alabama, demons and birds, mechanics,
    journalists, opera singers, the pure contralto singing in the organ loft, the
    noiseless, patient spider, the carpenter dressing his plank, the driver with his

interrogating thumb, the Good Grey poet camouflaged in the en-masse
searching for the cradle of liberty endlessly rocking;

*Out of the roughs, a kosmos,* all of my illegitimate word-children eating, drinking,
breeding, probing the darkness of our Captain's continuous assassination,
transformed into military scientists, impersonal, technological astronauts,
pursuing happiness into time, space, earth shrinking to a tiny orange below
us, up, up with "oceanic, variegated, intense, practical energy," to land in
triumph on the moon where, suddenly, down the ladder "disorderly fleshly and
sensual," I emerge singing to the moon's wasteland the Song of Myself.

# Walt Whitman at the Irish Festival, Syracuse, New York
## Four Snapshots

### I.

He hugs each policeman in turn,
and they laugh and turn a deep American red
beneath their blue caps.

### II.

He dances a jig with an old man
and a young girl
and a man inexplicably dressed
in a horned Viking helmet
and Scottish tartan kilt.
Sweat beads on his forehead
and his white beard tosses like a wave.
He dances badly, and long
into the night.

### III.

A man hawks buttons saying,
"Kiss me, I'm Irish."
He kisses him.

### IV.

He jumps the stage
(we did not know he played the mandolin)
to sing a song. It is a song no one
has heard before, and yet the band
remembers how to play it.
Everyone knows the words,
and everyone dances.

# Last Days in Camden

I

Days of calm. An invalid's mild diversions.
The pony cart, his present from admirers,
has the lame oldster trotting gamely round
his down-at-the-heels neighborhood once more.
It puts high color back into his face.
Jaunts of a few blocks cheer him. Reins in hand,
he tastes the freedom of a few years back,
when he could ramble far out of town, and did:
say, down the coast on a sunny winter's day
to limp sturdily up and down the beach,
tolerably like the ones he wandered
mile on mile in his Paumanok boyhood
(or like one that slips into his dreams
night after night, its flat, deserted stretch
passive under the crash and yank of combers).

Summers were better still. Hospitable waters
beckoned him convalescent to the woods
back of the Staffords' farm on Timber Creek.
There he would cast his clothes aside and wrestle
with a young sapling, leaning his whole weight
against its springy stem, trying to feel
a green suppleness stealing by mere contact
into his dragging limbs.
                              He squelched in ooze
of his favorite rivulet, rinsed his mud bath off
in a clear spring, then sprawled in a camp chair
to take the sun, bucknaked but for a wide-brimmed
straw hat. Slate-colored dragonflies in pairs
hovered close to his nose, inspecting him.

Sometimes he broke the silence of the woods
by singing songs he'd picked up from the army,
or from the just-freed slaves. He made
the cedars ring, an American Silenus
loafing at ease in his triumphant, improvised
western New Jersey spa. Edenic hours
pencilled just as limpidly as they passed.
Casual daybook entries burgeoning into
*Specimen Days*. . . .
                              Taking a corner now
at a terrific clip, he lurches, chuckles,
chokes up on the reins. His friends wonder:
had he ever driven before? A graybeard child,
thrilling to a new toy . . .
                              Then later strokes
cut back his territory. His rig idles.
The little horse, with no way to earn his oats,
is sold at last. His outings, much less frequent,
now have to be less heady. Warren, the wiry,
mustached, cardiganed, indispensable nurse,
bumps him down to the docks in a rickety
rattan wheelchair. There he watches coal boats
smudging by, and the everladen ferry
he once rode back and forth on half the night
just to look up at stars. Tug boats mewl,
cargoes jostle on and off of barges.
All rivers are one river. Now he looks
blinking across the brown wash of the Delaware,
inhales, resigned, the air he calls "malarial."
Time to go back. His wheels jounce on pier planks.


II


His cramped house sits on Mickle Street, an area
destitute of charm and, frankly, destitute.
An upstairs front room, homely with iron stove

and sprigged wallpaper, serves as bedroom, study,
and a salon to bands of devotees
come to receive the latest oracle.
Brash young men, the anti-Victorian vanguard,
herald his birthdays with fanatic zeal,
cosseting him with oysters and champagne.
He indulges them. He indulges himself,
as far as strength permits. Idolatry
carries vexations, though. He sags a bit
under the growing burden of their hopes
for the wonderful, unbuttoned twentieth century
that he won't live to see: a world redeemed
from priestcraft and hypocrisy, made happy
by universal suffrage and free love.
Mail will go faster (just the other day
someone sent him a little pasteboard box full
of orange buds, still fresh, from Florida).
Human relations will be governed by
the gospel of his verse and no doubt also
the wisdom of phrenology. He muses,
feeling his bumps with gentle, probing fingers.
Just as he was told: "Adhesiveness,
Amativeness, Self-Esteem, Sublimity"
all bulk large beneath his grizzled mane.

In between delphic interviews he dozes
in his big chair by the window, writes
snatches of verse, little squibs for the papers,
almost managing to ignore the reek
of the fertilizer plant across the river,
the chuff and rattle of the trains that pass
a hundred yards away and, when they don't,
on Sundays, sour Methodist steeple bells,
crass opponents of everybody's peace.
Papers and books heap round him on the floor.
He stirs them with his cane, or reaches down
now and again to riffle through the mess.

By a slow, unpremeditated system
of crossfiling, items migrate to the top.
Accolades from Swinburne, from Rossetti,
pleasant regards from Tennyson, fervent
declarations of love from female votaries
offering to conceive his child on some
fortunate mountaintop and save mankind.
Emerson's letter, lost for years, crops up,
tendering in its prim, Spencerian hand
thanks for the astonishing gift of *Leaves*:
"I greet you at the beginning of a great career."


III


Photograph after photograph, his countenance
gives nothing away. He knows and says it:
"There is something in my nature *furtive*
like an old hen!" How many prize eggs lie
clandestine in the hedgerows of the past?
His hooded, sunken eyes at last look back
and cannot see through his own snarled webs
to find those clutches lovingly concealed.
Nor can his biographers do better:
searches for the six illegitimate children
scattered supposedly through the south yield nothing.
A mystery unto himself and others,
he lets the camera catch him if it can.

Less than a year before his death he sits
a last time for his good friend Mr. Eakins.
Paints laid aside, the savage Philadelphian
stoops under his black hood, tweaks the bulb,
and frames Walt by the window in May sunlight.
A long exposure. But the subject is
accustomed to the discipline of sitting.
Here he is Prospero with his spells disowned,

or a Hasidic sage in contemplation,
or a retired Santa Claus who seems
half-transfigured in the window-light
which sets each wispy filament of blanched
prophetic beard to glowing. He leans back
against the darker, draping shagginess
of a wolfskin, wild mate to his repose.
Spring no longer lends heat to his flesh.
He waits here, well wrapped up, for what will come.

Waits with an old lover's tingling patience.
Whatever "furtive" (his word) human fumblings
he may have hid from others, from himself,
his true secret was something else, and hidden
like Poe's purloined letter, in plain sight.
Forget the baffled courtships of young laborers,
shy gifts of rings, and letters of endearment
tapering off as one by one the protégés
grew up, branched out, got married. This was not
what brought a skip and quickening to his pulse.
It was not sex but "heavenly death" which drew
his fascinated ardor all his life.
Faceless itself, reflecting all men's faces,
it held him, murmurous, many-lipped, enticing,
androgynous, a depth waiting unsounded,
into which one could slip without a ripple.
It overtook his soul in childhood,
saying its name to him on the night beach,
calling out in the tumbling of the waves.
Later it came back like a tide to steep
the rough-hewn hospitals of the Secession War.
Washed in the blood and tears of his new calling,
he sat by day and night beside the beds
of shattered soldiers, sponging at their brows,
writing their last words down in letters home.
Sometimes he helped to fold their finished hands
and walked behind the stretchers borne foot forward,

the cots already stripped for the new wounded.
Watchful, he marked the end as calm, maternal,
infinite in its welcome to desire.
This was the vision kept as counterweight
to every other force which stirred this kosmos.
So he declared his interest more than once.
Wildly out of context, for example,
in a prose dithyramb to democracy:
"In the future of these States must arise poets
immenser far, and make great poems of death."
Or is it out of context after all?
It may be just that longing for surcease,
a huge oblivion in or over nature,
which makes his writings most American.


IV


The deathbed scene, so cherished by an earlier
century when the practice was to ebb
and cozily expire at length, at home,
played itself out on Mickle Street with some
distinctive variations. Standing in
for the extended, hand-wringing family were
disciples trading off day and night shifts,
crank journalists, male nurses, amanuenses
jotting his few words down when he could not
manage his colored pencils any more.
Appetite failed in him. The last three days
he took nothing but small sips of milk punch.

After they moved him to "a water-bed"
(startling to learn they had a thing like that
in 1892) his ragged breathing
softened, and seemed to give him much less pain.
He heard the sound of water under him
swelling and lapsing, cradling his weight,

and gave himself up to it with a smile.
It was in keeping — wasn't it? — with his style:
ample, undulant, massing and lulling back,
penned simulacrum of the sea that shaped it. . . .
When he stopped breathing suddenly, his heart
("a very strong organ with him") continued
to beat ten minutes more. The camerados
watched him on his way to fathoming this:
"different from what any one supposed, and luckier."

# Walt Whitman at Bear Mountain

*. . . life which does not give the preference to any other life, of any
previous period, which therefore prefers its own existence. . . .*
— Ortega y Gasset

Neither on horseback nor seated,
But like himself, squarely on two feet,
The poet of death and lilacs
Loafs by the footpath. Even the bronze looks alive
Where it is folded like cloth. And he seems friendly.

"Where is the Mississippi panorama
And the girl who played the piano?
Where are you, Walt?
The Open Road goes to the used-car lot.

"Where is the nation you promised?
These houses built of wood sustain
Colossal snows,
And the light above the street is sick to death.

"As for the people — see how they neglect you!
Only a poet pauses to read the inscription."

"I am here," he answered.
"It seems you have found me out.
Yet, did I not warn you that it was Myself
I advertised? Were my words not sufficiently plain?

"I gave no prescriptions,
And those who have taken my moods for prophecies
Mistake the matter."

Then, vastly amused — "Why do you reproach me?
I freely confess I am wholly disreputable.
Yet I am happy, because you have found me out."

A crocodile in wrinkled metal loafing . . .

Then all the realtors,
Pickpockets, salesmen, and the actors performing
Official scenarios,
Turned a deaf ear, for they had contracted
American dreams.

But the man who keeps a store on a lonely road,
And the housewife who knows she's dumb,
And the earth, are relieved.

All that grave weight of America
Cancelled! Like Greece and Rome.
The future in ruins!
The castles, the prisons, the cathedrals
Unbuilding, and roses
Blossoming from the stones that are not there. . . .

The clouds are lifting from the high Sierras,
The Bay mists clearing.
And the angel in the gate, the flowering plum,
Dances like Italy, imagining red.

# Whitman Pinch Hits, 1861

After six months of wandering Whitman found himself
at the edge of a Long Island potato farm in early fall.
He saw a squad of young men at sport on sparse grass.
Looking up, he saw a few stray geese rise and circle back
north as though confused by the sudden Indian summer,
then looked down to study cart tracks cut deep into mud.
Weary of his own company, shorn of appetite, he thought
it would be sweet to sit awhile beside this field and watch
the boys in their shabby flannel uniforms playing ball.
Caught between wanting to look at them and wanting
them to look at him, he could not tell from this distance
if the torn and faded blues they wore were soldier's clothes
or baseball clothes. But he loved the rakish tilt of their caps
and cocky chatter drifting on the mid-day air. He had seen
the game played before, in Brooklyn, on a pebbled patch
laid out beside the sea, and thought it something young,
something brotherly for the frisky young and their brothers
to do in the shadow of civil war. That seemed two lifetimes
ago, not two years. The face he could no longer bear to find
in a mirror looked now like this island's ploughed ground.
Time does turn thick, Whitman thought, does press itself
against a man's body as he moves through a world torn apart
by artillery fire and weeping. Without knowing it happened,

he settled on a rise behind the makeshift home, moving
as he moved all year, a ghost in his own life. He should write
about baseball for the *Eagle*, or better still, make an epic poem
of it. The diamond chalked on grass, stillness held in a steady
light before the burst of movement, boys with their faces open
to the sky as a struck ball rose toward the all-consuming clouds.
But it was the sound that held him rapt. Wild, musical voices
punctuated by a pock of bat on ball, then the dropped wood

clattering to earth, grunts, everyone in motion through the air,
the resistant air, and then the lovely laughter. Whitman laughed
with them, a soundless gargle. The next batter staggered and fell,
drunk, his chin tobacco-splattered, laughing at his own antics
as he limped back to the felled tree where teammates sat.
They shook their heads, ignoring the turned ankle he exposed
for them to admire. Suddenly all eyes turned toward Whitman

where he lounged, propped on one elbow, straw hat tilted
to keep the sun from his neck, on the hill that let him see
everything at once. They beckoned. They needed Whitman
to pinch hit, to keep the game going into its final inning.
The injured batter held his stick out, thick end gripped in his fist,
and barked a curse. Whitman sat up, the watcher summoned
into a scene he has forgotten he did not create. They beckoned
and he came toward them like a bather moving through
thigh-high breakers, time stopping and then turning back,
letting him loose at last amid the spirits that greeted him
as the boys pounded his back, as they turned him around
and shoved him toward the field. In his hands, the wood
felt light. He stood beside the folded coat that represented
home, shifted his weight and stared at the pitcher who glared
back, squinting against the sun, taking the poet's measure.

# With Walt Whitman at Fredericksburg

*After Louis Simpson*

I have brought the twittering flags old bear-hug,
the swaying noose you admired at the end
of the 13th Brooklyn muskets sashaying
down Broadway, everybody's intended girl
swooning, Jesus, for the grandeur of it.

I have brought a tumbler of spring water
for the sipping if your brother George lives.

I see you and Simpson stepping carefully through
wreckage, the hacked-off arms, useless with Masonic
rings, for God's sake, shining like used-car lots.
The arms are so American, like parts junked
before the expiration of their longevity.
This is no joke for Velsor Brush to peddle.

I have brought a red handkerchief
for our mouths. Godalmighty, the stink grows.

I've come here like you to pick a way to the heart
of the business, tracing out what ripples I can,
skirting blood pooled like knocked-over
coffee on my own sunny backporch. But
I see you and Simpson arm wrestling
in a lantern's moon, sighing out
the lonely words of America's losses.

I wish I could say it was December 13, 1862,
but the faces of young men I see aren't Christ,
*dead and divine, and brother of all,* though
they wear the green clothes of Park Rangers,
the polite smile of Toledo, and one
thinks you sold him a Buick.

Isn't it for them we threw the noose in a can?
I gave George's water to a small boy found
by his mother in time, the life saved
he thought lost, which he will lose again.

If you lay your body down in this Virginia green,
you feel the quick shadows of tourists, the whispers
that zing in your stomach like miniballs or
knee-high bees. Loafing like this
you can hear the freeway moaning under ground
dry and beige as free-shrunken coffee,
or look up into the drained, tossing leaves
of October. Alone on a stolen Army blanket

I've stretched out a long time here
to dig from a bright afternoon the glazed eyes
of anyone whose temple, as I touch it to clean
away the smear of ice, breaks my heart.

At dusk I may be the only one left to drift
down Marye's Heights where the Rappahannock mist rolls
over rocks humped like bodies, little dunes
inside which a black tide I cannot see
goes on rising and falling. I want

to tell you how progress has not changed us much.
You can see breaking on the woods the lights
of cars and the broken limbs glow
in the boomed rush of traffic that chants
*wrong, wrong, wrong, wrong.*

# When Helen Keller Spoke

*(Walt Whitman Dinner, 1918)*

After others had said their say,
Some striving for wit,
Some exploiting their own penetration, psychology, cleverness,
Others heavily impressive,
She arose, Helen Keller,
Who never hears her own voice,
Nor any voice,
Who never sees the sun, the fields, the streams,
Nor any human face,
Whose hands alone, sensitive as antennae,
Convey to her imprisoned brain all it can know
Of life, of language, and of human thought;
She arose, and out of her changeless darkness and inner silence
Spoke.

With sightless eyes almost fixed, and void of expression,
She stood and made her lips, laboriously taught, utter words,
Words that came forth colorless, monotonously chanted,
Difficult to understand, for she could not sing the customary tunes of language,
Yet words that were every one a triumph, an achievement, a wonder,
For they uttered the soul of one who had out-generaled fate
And become a great woman.

Unlike the other speakers, she did not strive for rhetoric,
She did not stoop to wit or cleverness,
She did not elaborate commonplaces;
It would have been marvelous to hear her say that grass is green,
Or that music is sweet,
Or that she had learned to read Mother Goose;
But, under her terrible handicap, she had traveled far —
Denied the fundamental opportunity that is everyone's,

The use of hearing, sight, familiar speech,
She had become a person of culture, of trained mind,
The mistress of many languages, of the circle of the sciences, of philosophy itself;
Nor was she merely all this —
She alluded to herself as a Liberal,
She was one helping to bear the burden of the world.

She was talking of Walt Whitman,
Whom millions know but as a name,
And thousands mis-know through narrowness and ignorance,
And she said of him
That many are blind to his vision,
Deaf to his message, —
But she, though sightless, was not blind to it,
And, though dwelling in soundlessness, she was not deaf —
"He has opened many windows in my dark house,
"He makes me aware of the stars, the sunshine, the sea,
"And the wonderful night."

And, as she spoke,
Some who had ears became aware
That they heard not the music she could hear,
And, having eyes, they saw not the glories that were present to her.
Awed, silent, moved with humility and self-reproach,
They listened to Helen Keller's chanting strange voice,
That voice from beyond some dark mysterious barrier,
Watched upon her lips and unseeing eyes an expression of her ecstatic raptness,
And, when she sat down, burst into loud plaudits,
Which she could not hear.

# For You, Walt Whitman

Here is a message for you — the whole world sent it,
or maybe a ghost on radar, maybe lichen
growing on a stone. I'll try to read it —
it says there's a storm out there, there's a larger world
more gray than this one, and the storm is coming. I read
the message carefully: some day, and soon, not even
the lichen may speak, and even the ghost be gone,
and maybe even the large gray world you were standing on.

# from "Hot Dog"

VIII.

                            I followed Whitman
through half of Camden, across on the ferry and back
to Water Street; I lay down on his bed
and pushed my hand against the wall to bring
the forces back into my arms; I sang
something from *Carmen*, something from *La Bohème*,
and held my right hand up in the old salute
as music from my favorite regiment
came through the window glass as if to translate
not only the dust of those marching feet but the pails
of lopped-off arms and legs. I lay there thinking,
when I was dead — when he was dead — there would be
ten or more diseases, God knows what
they'd find if they cut him open, consumption, pneumonia,
fatty liver, gallstones, spongy abscesses,
collapsed lungs, tuberculosis of the stomach,
swollen brains. I lay there thinking his death
was lovely, just what he wanted. Mickle Street
was filled with people, for half a day, they stood
in front of the house and walked inside to stare
at the corpse. Thousands followed him to the grave
and filled up the giant tent or crowded the grass
around the tent, the grass he loved, the handkerchief,
the uncut powdered hair. How cunning it was
for them to walk on his head, he with that haircut,
he with that lotion, he whose grass kept growing
through all the speeches. Ingersoll was there —
he knew he would be — but he couldn't speak like the others
on the little bird going up and up; some Williams

you do not know read from Isaiah and Jesus
and later from Confucius and Gautama and Plato,
and someone spoke on the teaching and someone other
spoke on the immortality. Whitman lay there,
as far as I know, thinking about his house
and the ugly church across the street and the trains
banging and screeching a block away and all that
coal smoke and soot and the sweet odor that blew
across the river from the huge house of shit
on the Philadelphia side, but that was anyhow
the thing he loved, that shit, *n'est-ce pas?* — or he thought
of the day he spent with Burroughs walking in the sand
and smelling the ocean, how it was empty, it was
September already, the end of September, there was
much and copious talk, Whitman himself
was like the sea, he himself saw this lying
in the sand, his talk was sealike, Burroughs
himself saw it, Whitman thought the sea
was something beyond all operas — a little excessive;
he loved the surf the most, the hiss in southern
New Jersey sixty miles from Camden — he *was*
the sea, he knew that, though they dropped the dirt
now, they passed the shovel, someone threw
some pebbles, someone threw a flower, that was
the last time he would wander, what was the last
good thought? I ask this myself in Whitman's bed
after four hours of driving, after staring
out at his yard, he struggles with this, maybe
the hissing behind his poems, he likes that, he smiles —
a crumbling, sort of — maybe adhesiveness
again, he favored that word, or maybe
the world of matter, that would be good now, or how
he loved loose fish or how he hated that Concord —
was that uplifting enough? — maybe his room
on Mickle Street, the pile of papers, maybe
Oscar Wilde's visit, a dear young man, though Swinburne
he was a traitor, and he was a coward, how could he

understand his theory of women anyhow,
that Swinburne, there was a bird somewhere that rattled
as he did, boring, boring, he misunderstood
death, he was too weary — how could he call
Walt Whitman's Venus a drugged Hottentot
or Walt Whitman's Eve a drunken apple-woman
sprawling in the gutter? Walt Whitman loved
women, look how he grieved in the city deadhouse
alone with the poor dead prostitute, he called her
a house once full of passion and beauty, he called her
a dead house of love; and look how he spoke to that other,
how he made an *appointment* with her, "liberal and
lusty as nature," that's what he said; and how
he put his arm around the pimpled neck
of another as if she were a *comrade*; most,
how he praised the female form, she the gate
of the body, she the gate of the soul; some bastard
or other said he was cold, he said Walt Whitman
had too much distance, he the poet of touch,
he who wrote about love-juice, he who wrote
about lips of love and thumb of love and love
spendings and amorous pourings, he said that he
was distant, he of the swelling elate and he
who sang the song of procreation, he said
that women were only vessels to him, he said
there never was either passion *or* friendship, no woman
had ever hung her arm idly over his
shoulder and no woman died for love, her heart
pounding, not for him; but what about
the breath? And what about mad filaments
and negligent falling hands? Mostly he loved them
when they were tall and gray-haired, or he loved them
when they were flushed and uberous, he was
undissuadable; he hated the bastard,
he lay there hating — so what? so what? — Wasn't
democracy itself a *femme*, didn't they know that?
Didn't they know he wanted them as partners,

to swim and wrestle and shoot? They were comrades
too, or could be, he was thinking now
of how they fought, and he was thinking of how
he talked, how he was garrulous; but he was
clean, that was important. He thinks of the spray
at night on the ferry coming back to Camden;
he thinks of his own tenderness and he thinks
of his stubbornness, obstinancy Mrs. Stafford
called it, but most of all he thinks, even here —
wherever it is — of what the *person* is —
he had created his own person and now
he was loyal to that person. His last
good thought was how he scattered blossoms, I called them,
he said, O blossoms of my blood! O slender
leaves, you burn and sting me, it is your roots
I love, it is this death I love, I called it
exhilarating, twice now, out of my breast
the dark grass grew, I will never utter a call
only their call, put your hand in mine,
incline your face. Do you remember the body?
Do you remember lawlessness? I turned
around to face the window, that is the chair
that Wilde sat in, that is the table that Burroughs
drank his tea from, though probably not; the church
is gone, there is a huge county jail
across the way, the sweet smell of shit
from Philadelphia is gone, the soot
and smoke are gone, the ferry goes back and forth
only to the new blue-and-white aquarium,
and there is a thing called "Mickle Towers" two blocks
down, and acres of grass now and empty bottles —
that at least hasn't changed; I hiss one word
from my Phoenician, the bed is too narrow, a bird
is actually singing out there.

# Briefly Eavesdropping on
# Walt Whitman, Virginia, 1863

Officer Adolphus Jay,
I've been helped by a hare

that charged the ground littered with the wounded,
a hare seeking a lane into the woods,

its powerful feet twirling its body round and round
in fear at the howls and cheers

the men subjected upon it. "Skee-daddle,
Johnny Reb. Skee-daddle!"

Boys I watched die later this evening
joined the hubbub, their laughter

as large as mine, tears
running down our cheeks like hickory water.

Officer Adolphus Jay,
tonight, because of a hare

I'll have no nightmares of wagons
endlessly bringing in the sick and dying,

the stacks of arms and legs
won't grow beyond such infernal heights.

The hare might even remind me how future years
will forget this war as they should,

a tiny consolation I'll whisper from now on
to each brave man I hold in my arms.

# Walt Whitman at Pfaff's
## A Fantasy

Belly to the bar, bare chest heaving under the open laces,
rough workshirt billowing from throat to rib, a comrade
tethered at either side — arms encircling rough-trade
on the right, a looped lorryman to the left — divas, bassos,
and tenors at the tables, sailors staggering blindly together,
arms akimbo and raucous voices raised, a furtive couple bent close
in the far corner — as anchored as an atom of breath at the creation
you sprawl, at ease, under the glowing gaslamps.

Outside this ring of light, Walt, this fire,
your fellow poets stand, faces pressed to the glass —
dazed and unable to enter, to chance the step. Nothing
but "sophisticated dancing masters," they're afraid
to be as much woman as man, equally angel and demon,
nurses of despair, scops of the street, singers of cacophony
and tuners of harmony, lovers of legs and buttocks, of the soft skin
at the neck's nape, of the squirmings of the toes, Walt, and flaps
of the tongue, of the backs of the knees and of the feet shifting in sawdust.

The free lunch ranged along the bar, does it stretch on,
as it must, forever? Why don't you speak? Why not talk to us now
and tell us of the war to come and of the singers to be, of how
the feet form and of how the baby wails just at the moment when the death-
rattle erupts in an old man's throat, Walt? Tell us of bird songs
and musical shuttles, of the sun rising to erase the night's shadow —
of the bridegroom's first glimpse of the beloved body.
Teach us how to walk out into the world again, open-eyed
and empty-pocketed, faces rounding into the circle of "yes" once more.

# An Apple from Walt Whitman

There's never been a poet where I live,
but I grew up in the shade of Whitman's name:
born in West Hills — our hills — he would have walked
our paths along the crest. I walked Whitman Road,
crashed the Whitman Drive-In, stole a book
from the sci-fi rack at the Melville-Whitman Pharmacy,
even played lacrosse against Whitman High;
we lost three times, the guys from Halfway Hollow,
to men with *Whitman* in white on their varsity jackets.

My mother tells a story about Thanksgiving,
back when kids went begging in rags and blackface:
how Carrie Wicks's sister said she got
an apple from Walt Whitman, right at his house,
an old man with a beard. The big kids laughed,
knowing the white-haired caretaker was no one.

I set no foot inside the Whitman House
nor *Leaves of Grass* till after I'd gone away,
but I'm better having grown up with the name,
the house and hills of a poet everyone knew,
a poet big enough in the mothers' stories
for a girl to believe he came to the door with a long
white beard and smiled and handed her an apple.

If a poet the size of Whitman named our few
square miles and a few in Jersey it's going to take
a lot more big ones to hand us all a welcome
sweet as a Thanksgiving apple from Walt Whitman,
white-haired care-taker, seed of mothers' stories,
Appleseed of our poetry: nourishment, shade.

# Walt Whitman Bathing

After his stroke, he would walk into the woods
On sunny days and take off all his clothes
Slowly, one plain shoe
And one plain sock at a time, his good right hand
As gentle as a mother's, and bathe himself
In a pond while murmuring
And singing quietly, splashing a while
And dabbling at his ease, white hair and beard
Afloat and still streaming
Down his white chest when he came wading ashore
Naked and quivering. Then he would pace
In circles, sometimes dancing
A few light steps, his right leg leading the way
Unsteadily but considerately for the left
As if with an awkward partner.

He seemed as oblivious to passersby
As he was to his bare body, which was no longer
A nursery for metaphors
Or a banquet hall for figures of self-praise
But a bedroom or a modest bed in that bedroom
Or the covers on that bed
In need of airing out in the sunlight.
He would sit down on the bank and stare at the water
For an hour as if expecting
Something to emerge, some new reflection
In place of the old. Meanwhile, he would examine
The postures of wildflowers,
The workings of small leaves, holding them close
To his pale eyes while mumbling inaudibly.
He would dress then, helping
His left side with his right as patiently
As he might have dressed the wounded or the dead,
And would lead himself toward home like a dear companion.

# For Whitman

I have observed the learned astronomer
telling me the mythology of the sun.
He touches me with solar coronas.
His hands are comets with elliptical orbits, the
excuses for discovering planet X.

Lake water shimmering in sunset light,
and I think of the whitewashed dome of discovery
hovering over the landscape
wondering what knowledge does for us
in this old and beautiful un-knowing world.
     Yes,
         I would
rather name things
than live with wonder
or religion.

What the astronomer does not understand about poetry
is the truth of disguise.
That there are many names for the same phenomenon.
Love being
the unnamed/
the unnameable.

## On Walt Whitman's Birthday

O strategic map of disasters, hungry America
O target for the song, the jouncing poem,

                                      the protest

A long imperfect history shadows you
Let all suffering, toil, sex &
sublime distractions go recorded
Let the world continue to breathe

It's simple: a woman gets up & stretches
The world is her mirror & portal too

(Whitmanic morning task: wake the country to itself )

# The Good Grey Poet

Look to your words, old man,
for the original intelligence, the wisdom
buried in them. Know however that it
surfaces when it will. Perfect comrades
words have been, constant like few others
in your loneliness. But they too have a life,
a time, of their own to mature. Experiencing
the slow, essential music of their natures,
they must go their ways as you go yours.

After so many throes, so many convulsions,
not only a war that threatened to tear
your world to pieces, the world you had
most ambitiously dreamed, all the pieces
of bodies you had seen stacked under a tree,
the maggots working overtime, but deaths
accumulating of those dearest to you,
politics, conviviality, love, the rest
at last exhausted, do you not hear hints
from the vantage point of what you've become?

Your ideal, you wrote a healthy time ago
to guide yourself, was Merlin: "strong
& wise & beautiful at 100 years old."
Strong & wise since "his emotions &c are
complete in himself. . . . He grows, blooms,
like some perfect tree or flower, in Nature,
whether viewed by admiring eyes or in
some wild or wood entirely unknown."

For your liver fattening, the cyst ripening
in your adrenal, the left lung collapsed,
the right perhaps an eighth suitable
for breathing, a big stone rattled round
in your gall bladder (righter than you knew,
you were — and even at the time you wrote,
rock-bottom feelings under you, your poems —
truly incorporating gneiss!), the ball
of string tangled in the gut like a clue
to knit up all contrarieties, you must be
more and more yourself.
                                        Often, leaning
against a ferry rail, the sea your company,
your words beat out a rhythm so continuous
inside your body that you hardly noticed it,
content to let its current carry you along,
wherever it took you your place.
                                        Now
you, who thought — sufficient stores laid in —
that your awareness had already pierced
the distant future, view these phrases
and that rhythm, still pursuing its course,
as any stranger might.
                                        Your doubt does not
surprise. Who can miss the unexpected things
emerged to startle you, even waking shame
and fear?
                        But then you surely realize
how lucky you are, not only to have them,
these words, striking out on their own,
bearded with faces you scarcely recognize,
refusing to bend to your wishes or regrets,
refusing to acknowledge you in any way,
but to be able to use them — most because
they refuse — to measure that essential music
as it, and at its own sweet pace, moves on

to find the latest version of the truth
in the changes it is making.
                              Beyond that,
your words work, and work for you, by what
they do to others, bringing you — this
from far-off continents — reports of pleasure,
love, the tender might your poems go on
gathering as they inspire it.
                              And those,
the first breezy verses informing the winds,
your words in all their youthful innocence,
become so different, yet so much themselves,
like fruits more and more are bearing, bearing
out their father tree.

# Walt Whitman Encounters the Cosmos with the Cats of New York

The cats of morning awaken, sultry and feral,
Ready to hunt, to mate, to kick some serious cat butt.
Their green and yellow eyes burst open as a child slits the top off a pumpkin.

The alley cat is awake; the garbage can, last night's refuge, is rudely up-ended.
The Vanderbilts' cat awakens on Vanderbilt's pillow.
It washes its face with a loud shlurping noise.
The Vanderbilts do nothing; they are terrified of the thing.
The farm cat is up and about, looking for breakfast;
It falls on the field mice like Basil the Bulgar-Slayer.
The actress's cat makes a nest in last night's costume.
It may as well go back to sleep. She won't be up
Until God knows when. The banker's cat is curled
In a neat little package; it purrs that interest is rising.
The mother cat moves her kittens from the back of the closet
To the fireplace, thinks better of it, moves half of them back,
Then sits in the hallway and says to hell with this motherhood business.

Bastet is walking the streets and I walk with her.
I, Walt Whitman, companion of cats, have become all cats.
I look behind the restaurants for scraps of fish.
I rub myself on the legs of total strangers;
They run off screaming. They are unaware of my secret.
My brothers and sisters and I are watching the East;
The sun only rose this morning
Because my people are watching.

# Walt Whitman

*Translated from the Chinese by Richard Terrill and Cheng Baolin*

He is simply chopping wood in my front yard.
I imagined him far less quiet,
like sunlight.
I have to squint to look at him.
I imagined him far less quiet,
not vaguely chewing a leaf of tobacco.
He is not a butterfly
or a spoon or a plate
lying under an oak in Louisiana.
I imagined him far less quiet.
So it's best for him to chop wood,
stand in my front yard, chop wood with a *crack*,
like sunlight
white and proud.
We squint our eyes to look at him.

# Walt Whitman in Alabama

Maybe on his way to Gadsden,
Queen City of the Coosa,
to speak with the pilots
and inland sailors, to cross the fords
Jackson ran with blood or meet the mayor
who bought the ladies' favors with river quartz,
maybe east from some trip west to see
or returning north from New Orleans
or just lost in those years after The War
as legend has it, after the bannings,
when he'd grown tired of puffs and plates,
after he'd grown the beard and begun
to catch things there he had to walk off
or sing unwritten, maybe when the open road,
opened on mockingbirds two and two —
no one knows, though the stories have him here
recapturing Attalla, shaking poems from his hair
on the steps of local churches. Maybe
it was the end of many letters, the last
of hospital days, another sleight
to make his hand come alive
when he couldn't bring some Southron home.
I see him there remembering his poems,
his back to the door, singing
out to the garden of the world,
the tropical spring of pine and jasmine,
how wondrous it was the pent-up river
washed to green their farms, the creeks swole
with mountain dew to sprout the corn,
herbage of poke and collard,
spinach and bean, to wash the roots

of every leaf to come. But more
I wonder what he did not say,
whether the doors were closed on the room
where none thought Jesus ever naked,
whether he went down Gadsden's Broad
to the bluff where a hundred years thence
someone fabled a child lost from the arms
of his Hispanic mother and almost saved
by a cop who brought from his pocket
a shirt's worth of proof before the woman
vanished with her English, before the psychics
started rowing down the channel
to listen for the baby's dreams — all years after
the whorehouses, the fires, Reconstruction
and true religion came, after **Whitman** said his piece
and left the country to its mayors,
its wars and local dramas, Broad Street
and its theaters to opening and closing
and being torn down to photograph and rumor
where vaudeville variety traveled
in those years before the world became real
and history stilled, before the dams stalled
the yearly flood that washed the roots
and made new fields from catfish and shit
and the mountain dead, before
the sun in the tassels was wormed to shine,
before shine dried into the hills
with the snakes, the poetry, the legend.
I imagine him here in the different city,
bathing in the yellow light as the river slips
beneath the bridge, flickering like a candle
or like the body or like the bodies
lit up with gasoline and beer, tremble of taillights,
while the statue of the Civil War heroine
points fingerless down Broad, down the stream
of headlamps and embers of burning weed,
a congregation in which his secrets and his song

would be unwelcome, though he slake
some secret thirsts, his orotund voice
tune our ears to the river's whisper,
a baby cradled in branches
deep beneath the bridge.
Its ribs filter the Coosa's brown.
Its arms raise the crops.
And every night it whispers the town
in some new forgotten tongue.

# Notes on Contributors

Sherman Alexie's collections of poetry include *One Stick Song*, *The Man Who Loves Salmon*, *The Summer of Black Widows*, *Water Flowing Home*, *Old Shirts & New Skins*, *First Indian on the Moon*, and *The Business of Fancydancing*. His novels and collections of short fiction include *The Toughest Indian in the World*, *Indian Killer*, *Reservation Blues*, and *The Lone Ranger and Tonto Fistfight in Heaven*. Alexie also co-wrote the screenplay for the movie *Smoke Signals*, based on his short story "This Is What It Means to Say Phoenix, Arizona." He lives in Seattle, Washington.

Eugénio de Andrade is Portugal's best-known living poet as well as its most translated living writer. He received the Portuguese Writers Association's most distinguished award, the Lifetime of Literature Prize. *Solar Matter*, *Memory of Another River*, *Inhabited Heart*, and *The Slopes of a Gaze* are collections of English translations of his poetry.

Aliki Barnstone is the author of four books of poems: *Wild With It*, *Madly in Love*, *Windows in Providence*, and *The Real Tin Flower* (introduced by Anne Sexton), which was published when she was twelve years old. She is the editor of two anthologies of women's poetry: *Voices of Light: Spiritual and Visionary Poems by Women from Around the World* and *A Book of Women Poets from Antiquity to Now*. She teaches at the University of Nevada at Las Vegas.

Cheng Baolin was born in Hubei Province, China, in 1962. His own first book of poems appeared in 1985, while he was still an undergraduate, and sold out its run of ten thousand copies in the first month. He has since published, in Chinese, three more collections of poems and two books of essays. Formerly literary editor of *Sichuan Daily*, he now lives in San Francisco and is editor of the *Literati*, a Chinese language arts magazine.

Tony Barnstone is the author of *Impure*, a collection of poems, and the editor of *Out of the Howling Storm: The New Chinese Poetry*; *Laughing Lost in the Mountains: Selected Poems of Wang Wei*; *The Art of Writing: Techniques of the Chinese Masters*; and *The Anchor Book of Chinese Poetry*. He teaches at Whittier College in California.

Willis Barnstone is the prolific poet and translator of more than forty-five collections of poetry, scholarship, translations, and memoir, including *Algebra of Night: New and Selected Poems, 1948–1998*; *The Other Bible*; *The Secret Reader: 501 Sonnets*; *With Borges on an Ordinary Evening in Buenos Aires*, a memoir and biography; *Sunday Morning in Fascist Spain*, a memoir; *The Poetics of Translation*; *Sappho and the Greek Lyric Poets*; and *To Touch the Sky: Poems of Mystical, Spiritual, and Metaphysical Light*. His literary translation of the New Testament is entitled *The New Covenant: The Four Gospels and Apocalypse*. He is Distinguished Professor of Comparative Literature, Spanish, and East Asian Cultures at Indiana University.

Marvin Bell divides his time among Iowa City, Iowa; Sag Harbor, New York; and Port Townsend, Washington. Among his sixteen collections of poems are *The Book of the Dead Man*, *Ardor*, and most recently *Nightworks: Poems 1962–2000*. He is Flannery O'Connor Professor of Letters at the University of Iowa, where he has taught for more than three decades. In March 2000 he was selected to be Iowa's first poet laureate.

Joe Benevento is a professor of English at Truman State University, where he teaches courses in American and Latin American literature and creative writing. He is the author of *Holding On*, a collection of poems.

Ted Berrigan was born in Providence, Rhode Island, in 1934. Among his more than twenty collections of poems are *The Sonnets*; *Bean Spasms* (with Ron Padgett and Joe Brainard); *Poems, In Brief*; *Red Wagon*; *So Going Around Cities: New & Selected Poems 1958–1979*; and *A Certain Slant of Sunlight*, published posthumously. He died in 1983. *Nice to See You: Homage to Ted Berrigan*, published in 1991, is a collection of essays, poems, and reminiscences by his many friends, recounting Berrigan's influence on the writers of his generation.

John Berryman received the Pulitzer Prize for *77 Dream Songs* in 1967. At the time of his death in 1972 at the age of fifty-seven, the number of dream songs had grown to 385. Among his collections of poetry are *Homage to Mistress Bradstreet*, *Berryman's Sonnets*, *Henry's Fate*, and *Collected Poems: 1937–1971*.

Robert Bly's many books of poems include *Silence in the Snowy Fields*, *The Light Around the Body* — winner of the National Book Award — and most recently *The Night Abraham Called to the Stars* and *Eating the Honey of Words: New and Selected Poems*. Recent collections of translations include *The Half-Finished Heaven: The Best Poems of Tomas Tranströmer* and *The Lightning Should Have Fallen on Ghalib* (with Sunil Dutta). His essays have been collected in *Iron John*, *The Sibling Society*, *The Maiden King* (with Marion Woodman), and *American Poetry: Wildness and Domesticity*.

Jorge Luis Borges was born in Buenos Aires in 1899. Poet, essayist, and short story writer, he is one of the giants of twentieth-century world literature. He died in 1986. *Selected Poems*, *Collected Fictions*, and *Selected Non-Fictions* make his work available in English editions.

Michael Dennis Browne is the author of five collections of poems, most recently *You Won't Remember This* and *Selected Poems, 1965–1995*. Browne came to the United States from England in 1965; he currently teaches at the University of Minnesota and lives in Minneapolis. A new collection of poems, *What I Can't Tell You*, is forthcoming in 2004.

Joseph Bruchac is a writer and storyteller whose work often draws on his Abenaki Indian ancestry. Author of over ninety books for adults and young readers, his most recent collections of poetry are *Above the Line* and *Ndakinna, Our Land*. With his wife, Carol, he is the founder and co-director of the Greenfield Review Literary Center and the Greenfield Review Press, which has been publishing important work for more than thirty years.

Edward Byrne is the author of five collections of poems, including *Tidal Air*, *Along the Dark Shore*, and *The Return to Black and White*. He is professor of American literature and creative writing at Valparaiso University in Indiana, where he also serves as editor of the on-line journal *Valparaiso Poetry Review*.

Thomas Centolella is the author of *Views from Along the Way*, *Lights and Mysteries*, and *Terra Firma*. He teaches writing at the College of Marin and is a staff artist for the Goldman Institute on Aging. He makes his home in San Francisco.

Nicholas Christopher is the author of seven collections of poetry, including *Atomic Field: Two Poems* and *Creation of the Night Sky*; four novels, including *A Trip to the Stars* and *Franklin Flyer*; and a nonfiction book, *Somewhere in the Night: Film Noir and the American City*. He lives in New York City where he is professor in the Writing Division of the School of the Arts at Columbia University.

David Citino is professor of English and creative writing at Ohio State University. A former director of the Creative Writing Program and editor of the magazine the Journal, he is the author of eleven books of poetry, most recently *The Invention of Secrecy* and *The Book of Appassionata: Collected Poems*. He recently edited *The Eye of the Poet: Six Views of the Art and Craft of Poetry*.

Jonathan Cohen is a poet, translator of Latin American poetry, and essayist. Among his books are the translations of Roque Dalton's *Small Hours of the Night*, Pedro Mir's *Countersong to Walt Whitman and Other Poems*, and Ernesto Cardenal's *With Walker in Nicaragua and Other Early Poems*, and *Poems from the Islands*, a collection of his own poems. He currently lives in Manhattan and works on Long Island — close to Whitman's birthplace — at SUNY–Stony Brook, where he is writer-in-residence in the surgery department.

Gillian Conoley is the author of four collections of poetry: *Lovers in the Used World*; *Tall Stranger*, nominated for the National Book Critics Circle Award; *Beckon*; and *Some Gangster Pain*. Founder and editor of Volt, she is poet-in-residence at Sonoma State University and lives in the San Francisco Bay area.

David Cope is the author of four collections of poetry, including *Quiet Lives* and *On the Bridge*. He teaches Shakespeare, drama, and creative writing at Western Michigan University and Grand Rapids Community College, and has served on the summer faculty at Naropa University. He lives in Grandville, Michigan.

Betty Jean Craige is director of the Center for Humanities and Arts and University Professor of Comparative Literature at the University of Georgia. She is the author of *Lorca's Poet in New York* and translator of *The Poetry of Gabriel Celaya*; *Manuel Mantero*; and *Selected Poems of Antonio Machado*.

Bruce Cutler, former Adele M. Davis Distinguished Professor of Humanities and founding director of the Creative Writing Program at Wichita State University, is the author of numerous collections of prose and poetry, including *The Massacre at Sand Creek: Narrative*

*Voices* and *At War with Mexico: A Fictional Mosaic.* After his retirement from teaching, he resided in Santa Cruz, California, until his death in 2001.

Philip Dacey is the author of seven collections of poetry, including *The Deathbed Playboy* and *The Paramour of the Moving Air.* He teaches part-time at Southwest State University in Minnesota.

Toi Derricotte is the author of *Tender, Captivity,* and *Natural Birth,* all collections of poems, and a prose memoir, *The Black Notebooks: An Interior Journey.* She currently lives in Pittsburgh, Pennsylvania, where she teaches in the MFA in Writing Program at the University of Pittsburgh.

W. S. Di Piero's collections of poetry include *Skirts and Slacks, Shadows Burning, The Restorers,* and *The Dog Star.* His books of translation include Euripides's *Ion, The Ellipse: Selected Poems of Leonardo Sinisgalli, This Strange Joy: Selected Poems of Sandro Penna,* and Giacomo Leopardi's *Pensieri.* He is also the author of three collections of essays: *Shooting the Works: On Poetry and Pictures, Out of Eden: Essays on Modern Art,* and *Memory and Enthusiasm: Essays, 1975–1985.* He lives in San Francisco and is a professor of English at Stanford University.

Mark Doty is the author of six books of poems, including *Source, Sweet Machine, Atlantis,* and *My Alexandria,* winner of the National Book Critics Circle Award and a National Book Award finalist. His collections of prose include *Heaven's Coast: A Memoir* and *Firebird,* an autobiography. He teaches in the Creative Writing Program at the University of Houston.

Richard Eberhart's many collections of poems include *New and Selected Poems: 1930–1990* and *Maine Poems and Collected Poems: 1930–1986.* In 1966 he received the Pulitzer Prize for his *Selected Poems.*

Lynn Emanuel is the author of three books of poetry: *Hotel Fiesta; The Dig;* and *Then, Suddenly —.* She is professor of English at the University of Pittsburgh and director of the Writing Program.

Martín Espada's seventh poetry collection is *Alabanza: New and Selected Poems, 1982–2002.* Another collection, *Imagine the Angels of Bread,* won an American Book Award in 1996. Espada teaches at the University of Massachusetts–Amherst.

Dave Etter is the author of more than twenty-five collections of poems, including *Selected Poems, Sunflower County, How High the Moon,* and most recently *Next Time You See Me.* He lives in Lanark, Illinois.

Richard Fein is the author of five collections of poems, including *I Think of Our Lives: New and Selected Poems* and *Kafka's Ear.* He also has written *The Dance of Leah,* a memoir; *Robert Lowell,* a critical study; and *Selected Poems of Yankev Glatshteyn,* translations. He lives in Cambridge, Massachusetts.

Lawrence Ferlinghetti is the author of more than two dozen books of poetry, including *San Francisco Poems; How to Paint Sunlight; A Far Rockaway of the Heart; These Are My Rivers: New and Selected Poems, 1955–1993; Over All the Obscene Boundaries: European Poems and Transi-*

tions; and *A Coney Island of the Mind*, which has more than a million copies in print. He is also the author of eight plays and of the novels *Love in the Days of Rage* and *Her*. In 1994, San Francisco renamed a street in his honor, and in 1988 he was also named that city's first poet laureate. In 2000, he received the lifetime achievement award from the National Book Critics Circle. He resides in San Francisco, where he operates City Lights Publishers and the City Lights Bookstore.

Calvin Forbes teaches writing, literature, and jazz history at the School of the Art Institute of Chicago. His collections of poetry include *The Shine Poems*, *From the Book of Shine*, and *Blue Monday*.

Randall Freisinger is the author of *Plato's Cave*, *Hard Shadows*, and *Running Patterns*. Since 1977 he has lived in Michigan's Upper Peninsula where he teaches writing and literature at Michigan Technical University.

Daisy Fried is the author of *She Didn't Mean to Do It*, a collection of poems. She teaches writing at Haverford College in Pennsylvania and lives in Philadelphia.

Thomas Gannon is completing a doctorate in English at the University of Iowa on "avian alterity" in Romantic and Native American literatures. His e-anthology of avian poetry from Chaucer to the present can be viewed at *http://www.usd.edu/~tgannon/quindex.html*.

Suzanne Gardinier is the author of *The New World*, a collection of poems, and *A World That Will Hold All the People: Essays on Poetry and Politics*. She teaches at Sarah Lawrence College and lives in New York City.

Allen Ginsberg was born in Newark, New Jersey, in 1926. With William S. Burroughs, Neal Cassady, and Jack Kerouac, he became a leading figure of the Beat Generation. Among his numerous collections of poetry are *Howl and Other Poems*; *Kaddish and Other Poems*; *Reality Sandwiches*; *Wichita Vortex Sutra*; *The Fall of America: Poems of These States, 1965–1971*, winner of the National Book Award; *Collected Poems, 1947–1980*; *Selected Poems, 1947–1995*; *White Shroud: Poems, 1980–85*; *Cosmopolitan Greetings: Poems, 1986–1992*; and *Death and Fame: Last Poems, 1993–1997*. With Ann Waldman, he co-founded and directed the Jack Kerouac School of Disembodied Poetics at Naropa University in Colorado, and later he became a Distinguished Professor at Brooklyn College. He died in 1997 in New York City.

Jesse Glass is the author of *Against the Agony of Matter*, *Song for Arepo*, *Make Death Die*, and *The Book of Doll*. He is professor of American literature and history at Meikai University in Chiba, Japan, where he also makes his home.

Patricia Goedicke is the author of twelve collections of poetry, including *As Earth Begins to End*, *Invisible Horses*, *Paul Bunyan's Bearskin*, and *The Tongues We Speak*. She lives in Missoula, Montana, where she is professor of Creative Writing at the University of Montana.

Albert Goldbarth is Distinguished Professor of Humanities in the Department of English at Wichita State University. He is the author of over twenty collections of poetry, including *Saving Lives*, winner of the 2002 National Book Critics Circle Award, and *Heaven and Earth: A Cosmology*, winner of the 1991 National Book Critics Circle Award. He is also the author of *A Sympathy of Souls*, a collection of essays. He lives in Wichita, Kansas.

Beckian Fritz Goldberg is the author of several collections of poetry, including *The Book of Accident*, *Never Be the Horse*, and *In the Badlands of Desire*. She directs the MFA in Creative Writing Program at Arizona State University and lives in Carefree, Arizona.

David Graham is the author of six collections of poems, including *Accidental Blessings*, *Second Wind*, and *Magic Shows*. With Kate Sontag, he edited *After Confession: Poetry as Autobiography*, a collection of essays. He is professor of English at Ripon College in Wisconsin, where he teaches writing and literature.

Matthew Graham is the author of *New World Architecture* and *1946*, collections of poems. He teaches at the University of Southern Indiana, where he co-directs The Rope Walk Writers Retreat and is poetry editor of the *Southern Indiana Review*. He lives in Evansville, Indiana.

Jim Harrison is the author of numerous novels, novellas, collections of short stories, collections of poetry, essays, and screenplays, among them *The Raw and the Cooked*, *The Road Home*, *Wolf: A False Memoir*, *Legends of the Fall*, *Just Before Dark*, *Dalva*, *A Woman Lit by Fireflies*, *Julip*, *Will Write for Food*, and *The Shape of the Journey: New and Collected Poems*. For many years, he served as the food columnist for *Esquire* magazine. He divides his time between northern Michigan and southern Arizona.

William Heyen is professor of English and poet-in-residence at SUNY–Brockport, his undergraduate alma mater. His books of poetry include *Long Island Light*; *Erika: Poems of the Holocaust*; *The Host: Selected Poems, 1965–1990*; *Crazy Horse in Stillness*, winner of the 1997 Small Press Book Award for Poetry; and *Pig Notes & Dumb Music: Prose on Poetry*.

Edward Hirsch has published five books of poems, most recently *On Love* and *Earthly Measures*, and three collections of prose: *The Demon and the Angel: Searching for the Source of Artistic Inspiration*, *Responsive Reading*, and *How to Read a Poem and Fall in Love with Poetry*. He is a recipient of the National Book Critics Circle Award, and in 1998 a MacArthur Fellowship.

Daniel Hoffman has published ten books of poetry, including *Darkening Water* and *Hang-Gliding from Helicon: New and Selected Poems, 1948–1988*. His books of criticism include *Words to Create a World*; *Poe Poe Poe Poe Poe Poe Poe*, nominated for a National Book Award; *Form and Fable in American Fiction*; and *The Poetry of Stephen Crane*. He is Felix Schelling Professor of English Emeritus at the University of Pennsylvania and lives in Swarthmore, Pennsylvania.

Edwin Honig, poet and translator, has published ten books of poetry, eight books of translations, five books of criticism, and three books of plays. He has taught at Harvard and Brown University, where he started the Graduate Writing Program. In 1996, he was knighted by the king of Spain, and in 1986 by the president of Portugal, for his work in literary translation. He is emeritus professor at Brown University and lives in Providence, Rhode Island.

Paul Hoover is the author of seven poetry collections, including *Totem and Shadow: New & Selected Poems*; *Viridian*; and the book-length poem *The Novel*. He also has edited *Postmodern American Poetry: A Norton Anthology*, a collection of American avant-garde poetry since 1950. His novel *Saigon, Illinois* is based on his experiences as a conscientious objector working at a Chicago hospital during the Vietnam War. He is a founding member of The Poetry Center at the School of the Art Institute of Chicago and has been poet-in-residence at Columbia College, Chicago, since 1974. He divides his time between Chicago and his home near San Francisco.

Langston Hughes — poet, novelist, playwright, journalist, translator — was born in Joplin, Missouri, in 1902. Hughes's first book of poetry, *The Weary Blues*, was published by Alfred A. Knopf in 1926. At the center of the 1920s artistic movement known as the Harlem Renaissiance, Hughes is the author of numerous books of poetry, including *Fine Clothes to the Jew*, *Dear Lovely Death*, *The Dream Keeper and Other Poems*, *Scottsboro Limited*, *Shakespeare in Harlem*, *Montage of a Dream Deferred*, *Selected Poems*, *Ask Your Mama: 12 Moods for Jazz*, *The Panther and the Lash: Poems of Our Times*, and *Collected Poems of Langston Hughes*. Hughes died in 1967 in New York. The New York City Preservation Commission has given his home at 20 East 127th Street in Harlem historic landmark status. The city also renamed East 127th Street "Langston Hughes Place."

T. R. Hummer is the author of six collections of poems, including *Useless Virtues*, *Walt Whitman in Hell*, *The 18,000-Ton Olympic Dream*, and *Lower-Class Heresy*. Former editor of the *Kenyon Review* and *New England Review*, he currently lives in Athens, Georgia, where he is the editor of the *Georgia Review* at the University of Georgia.

David Ignatow was born in Brooklyn in 1914 and spent most of his life in the New York City area. He is the author of numerous books of poetry, including *Living Is What I Wanted: Last Poems*; *At My Ease: Uncollected Poems of the Fifties and Sixties*; *Against the Evidence: Selected Poems, 1934–1994*; and *New and Collected Poems, 1970–1985*. For many years he served as poetry editor of the *Nation*. In 1987, he was poet-in-residence at the Walt Whitman Birthplace Association. He died in 1997 at his home in East Hampton, New York.

Gray Jacobik is the author of three collections of poems: *Brave Disguises*, *The Surface of Last Scattering*, and *The Double Task*. She is professor of literature at Eastern Connecticut State University in Willimantic, and lives in Pomfret, Connecticut.

Juan Ramón Jiménez was born in Moguer, Spain, in 1881. He published his first book of poems, *Almas De Violeta*, when he was nineteen. He was associated with the literary group known as the "modernistas," which also included the poet Rubén Darió. He worked as an editor of several literary journals for many years. In 1936, as the result of the Spanish civil war, Jiménez left Spain for Puerto Rico and Cuba. In 1939, he came to the United States, where he lived until 1951. He then returned to Puerto Rico where he died in 1958, two years after receiving the Nobel Prize for Literature. His work is available in such English translations as *Selected Writings of Juan Ramón Jiménez*; *Three Hundred Poems, 1903–1953*; and *Light and Shadow: Selected Poems and Prose*.

Erica Jong — poet, novelist, and essayist — is best known for her seven best-selling novels, including *Fear of Flying, How to Save Your Own Life*, and *Fanny*. Her six collections of poems include *Fruits and Vegetables*; *Half-Lives*; *Loveroot*; and *Becoming Light: Poems, New and Selected*. Her mid-life memoir *Fear of Fifty* was an international best-seller. Her work has been translated into more than twenty-five languages. She lives in New York City.

John Judson is the author of several collections of poems, including *Three Years before the Braves Left Boston*. Founder and editor of Juniper Press and the poetry journal *Northeast* in 1963, Judson retired from teaching at the University of Wisconsin–LaCrosse, where he was professor of English. He continues to live in LaCrosse, Wisconsin.

Yusef Komunyakaa, born in Louisiana, is the author of several collections of poetry, including *Talking Dirty to the Gods*; *Pleasure Dome: New and Collected Poems, 1975–1999*; *Thieves of Paradise*, a finalist for the National Book Critics Circle Award; and *Neon Vernacular: New and Selected Poems, 1977–1989*, recipient of the Pulitzer Prize. He is also the author of *Blues Notes: Essays, Interviews, and Commentaries*. He lives in New York City and teaches at Princeton University.

Steve Kowit is best known for his writing manual, *In the Palm of My Hand*. He has translated Neruda's *Incitement to Nixoncide and Praise for the Chilean Revolution*. His most recent collection of poetry is *The Dumbbell Nebula*. He teaches at Southwestern College in Chula Vista, California.

Norbert Krapf is the author of *Bittersweet along the Expressway: Poems of Long Island*; *Blue-Eyed Grass: Poems of Germany*; and *Somewhere in Southern Indiana: Poems of Midwestern Origins*. He also is the editor/translator of *Beneath the Cherry Sapling: Legends from Franconia* and *Shadows on the Sundial: Selected Early Poems of Rainer Maria Rilke*. Prior to his retirement, he directed the C. W. Post Poetry Center of Long Island University, where he was a professor of English. He lives in Indianapolis, Indiana.

Mark Kraushaar's poems have appeared in many journals, including *Another Chicago Magazine, Beloit Poetry Journal, Gettysburg Review, Poetry East*, and *Shenandoah*. He lives in Madison, Wisconsin.

Philip Levine's numerous collections of poetry include *The Mercy*; *The Simple Truth*, winner of the Pulitzer Prize; *What Work Is*, winner of the National Book Award; *New Selected Poems*; *Ashes: Poems New and Old*, winner of the National Book Critics Circle Award; *7 Years from Somewhere*, winner of the National Book Critics Circle Award; and *The Names of the*

*Lost.* He has also published a collection of essays, *The Bread of Time: Toward an Autobiography.* He divides his time between Fresno, California, and Brooklyn, New York.

Larry Levis was born in Fresno, California, in 1946. His collections of poetry include *Wrecking Crew, The Afterlife,* and *The Dollmaker's Ghost.* Levis was director of the Creative Writing Program at the University of Utah, and from 1992 to 1996 a professor of English at Virginia Commonwealth University. He died in 1996. *Elegy,* his last collection of poems, was published posthumously in 1997.

Alexis Levitin, professor of English at SUNY–Plattsburgh, has translated nine volumes of Eugénio de Andrade's poetry from Portuguese into English, including *Dark Domain* and *Close to Speech.* He also is the translator into English of Egito Gonçalves's *News from the Blockade and Other Poems* and Carlos de Oliveira's *Guernica and other Poems.* In 1989, Levitin accompanied Eugénio de Andrade on his nationwide tour as his translator.

Federico García Lorca is considered by many to be the most influential and most important Spanish poet and dramatist of the twentieth century. Born in 1899, in Fuente Vaqueros, a small town near Granada, Lorca published his first book, *Impresiones y Viajes,* when he was just eighteen. In 1929, García Lorca visited New York. In July of 1936, shortly after civil war broke out in Spain, Lorca was arrested, jailed, and then murdered by Franco's Facists. His body was never recovered. His work is available in such English translations as *Lament for the Death of a Bullfighter and Other Poems, Poet in New York, Lorca and Jiménez: Selected Poems,* and *Selected Poems.* His plays include *The Blood Wedding* and *The House of Bernarda Alba.*

Thomas Lux is the author of several collections of poetry, among them *The Street of Clocks; New and Selected Poems, 1975–1995; The Blind Swimmer: Selected Early Poems, 1970–1975;* and *The Drowned River: New Poems.* A former poet-in-residence at Emerson College and a member of the writing faculty at Sarah Lawrence College, he is currently Bourne Professor of Poetry at Georgia Institute of Technology in Atlanta.

David Mason is the author of *The Country I Remember, The Buried Houses, Land without Grief,* and *Small Elegies,* all collections of poems; and *The Poetry of Life and the Life of Poetry,* a collection of essays. With Mark Jarman he is co-editor of *Rebel Angels: 25 Poets of the New Formalism,* and with John Frederick Nims co-editor of the fourth edition of *Western Wind: An Introduction to Poetry.* He teaches at Colorado College.

Lynne McMahon is the author of three collections of poems: *Sentimental Standouts, The House of Entertaining Science,* and *Devolution of the Nude.* She is professor of English at the University of Missouri in Columbia, Missouri.

Gary Miranda is the author of three collections of poems: *Turning Sixty, Grace Period,* and *Listeners at the Breathing Place.* He also has translated Rilke's *Duino Elegies,* and was awarded first prize from the Venice Arts International Screenplay Competition in 2001 for his original screenplay *Brothers.* He lives in Portland, Oregon.

Roger Mitchell is the author of seven books of poetry, the most recent of which are *Savage Beauty*, *Braid*, and *The World for Everything*. He is also the author of a book of nonfiction, *Clear Pond: The Reconstruction of a Life*. He divides his time between Bloomington, Indiana, where he teaches at Indiana University, and Jay, New York.

Judith Moffett is the author of ten books in several genres, including poetry, science fiction, literary criticism, creative nonfiction, and translations from the Swedish. Her most recent book is *The North! To the North!: Five Swedish Poets of the Nineteenth Century*. A former faculty member at the Iowa Writers' Workshop, she was a member of the English faculty at the University of Pennsylvania for fifteen years.

Stanley Moss makes his living as a private art dealer in Spanish and Italian old masters. Publisher and editor of Sheep Meadow Press, his most recent book is *A History of Color and Asleep in the Garden: New and Selected Poems*. He lives in Riverdale, New York.

Howard Nelson is the author of four collections of poetry, the most recent of which is *Bone Music*. He is also the author of *Robert Bly: An Introduction to the Poetry* and editor of *On the Poetry of Galway Kinnell: The Wages of Dying*. He edited *Earth, My Likeness: Nature Poems of Walt Whitman*, a selection of Whitman's nature poems with woodcuts. He is professor of English at Cayuga Community College in Auburn, New York, and lives in the Finger Lakes region of New York.

Howard Nemerov was born in 1920 in New York. He taught at Washington University where he was Distinguished Poet-in-Residence from 1969 until his death in 1991. Nemerov's many collections of poems include *Trying Conclusions: New and Selected Poems, 1961–1991* and *The Collected Poems of Howard Nemerov* (1977), which won the Pulitzer Prize, the National Book Award, and the Bollingen Prize. His novels include *The Homecoming Game*, *Federigo: Or the Power of Love*, and *The Melodramatists*. He served as poetry consultant to the Library of Congress in 1963 and 1964, and as poet laureate of the United States from 1988 to 1990.

Pablo Neruda — born Neftalí Ricardo Reyes Basoalto in southern Chile in 1904 — is considered by many to be Latin America's greatest poet. In 1933, Neruda was named Chilean consul in Buenos Aires, Argentina, and in 1939 Chilean consul to Mexico. In 1943, he was elected to the Senate, then joined the Communist Party. When the rightist Chilean government outlawed communism, Neruda was expelled from the Senate and went into hiding. Neruda's many awards included the International Peace Prize in 1950, the Lenin Peace Prize and the Stalin Peace Prize in 1953, and the Nobel Prize for Literature in 1971. He died of leukemia on September 23, 1973, in Santiago, Chile. Among his many collections of poems available in English translation are *Pablo Neruda: Selected Poems*; *100 Love Sonnets*; *Book of Questions*; *Twenty Love Poems: And a Song of Despair*; *Full Woman, Fleshly Apple, Hot Moon: Selected Poems of Pablo Neruda*; and *Neruda and Vallejo: Selected Poems*.

Sharon Olds is the author of six collections of poems, including *The Dead and the Living*, winner of the National Book Critics Circle Award, and most recently, *The Unswept Room*. She teaches in the Graduate Creative Writing Program at New York University and helps run the New York University workshop program at Goldwater Hospital on Roosevelt Island in New York. She was appointed New York State Poet Laureate for 1998–2000.

Anthony Piccione was born in Sheffield, Alabama, in 1939, and raised on Long Island. He taught English and creative writing at SUNY–Brockport until his death in 2001. His collections of poetry include *Anchor Dragging* and *Seeing It Was So*. A posthumous collection, *The Guests at the Gate*, was published in 2002, with a foreword by Robert Bly.

Stanley Plumly is the author of seven collections of poetry, including *Now That My Father Lies Down Beside Me: New and Selected Poems, 1970–2000*; *Out-of-the-Body Travel*, nominated for the National Book Critics Circle Award; *Giraffe*; and *In the Outer Dark*. He is Distinguished University Professor of English at the University of Maryland.

Ezra Loomis Pound was born in Hailey, Idaho, in 1885. His numerous collections of prose and poetry — as well as his work as editor — helped shape twentieth-century modernist poetry and poetics, perhaps more than any other person. He died in Venice, Italy, in 1972. "A Pact" first appeared in *Poetry: A Magazine of Verse* in 1913.

Edwin Arlington Robinson was born in 1869 in Head Tide, Maine, and in 1870 his family moved to Gardiner, Maine, the "Tilbury Town" of his poems. Robinson worked as a subway inspector for the city of New York, and when *Captain Craig and Other Poems* was published in 1902, it so impressed President Theodore Roosevelt that he offered Robinson a job in a U.S. Customs House. Other collections include *The Man Against the Sky*, and *Merlin*, *Lancelot*, and *Tristram*, a trilogy based on Arthurian legends, which won a Pulitzer Prize in 1928. Robinson was also awarded a Pulitzer Prize for his *Collected Poems* in 1922 and *The Man Who Died Twice* in 1925. He died in New York City in 1935. "Walt Whitman" was first published in 1897.

Larry Rottmann, a native Missourian and Vietnam War veteran, teaches journalism at Southwest Missouri State University in Springfield. He is working on a documentary about former U.S. Surgeon General Joycelyn Elders.

Ira Sadoff has published six collections of poetry, including *Grazing*, *Emotional Traffic*, and *Palm Reading in Winter*. He has also published a novel, *Uncoupling*, and *The Ira Sadoff Reader*, a collection of stories, poems, and essays. He currently teaches at Colby College, where he is Dana Professor of Poetry, and in the MFA Program at Warren Wilson College. He lives in Waterville, Maine.

Terrence Savoie has published poems in numerous magazines, journals, and anthologies, including *American Poetry Review*, the *Iowa Review*, the *Nebraska Review*, and *Poetry*. He lives in Davenport, Iowa.

James Schevill — poet, dramatist, and novelist — has taught at San Francisco State University and Brown University, where he is professor of English emeritus. His collections of poetry include *New and Selected Poems* and *The Complete American Fantasies*. He is also the author of *Collected Short Plays* and *Arena of Ants*, a novel. He lives in Berkeley, California.

Shane Seely is a recent graduate of the MFA program at Syracuse University, where he was awarded the Delmore Schwartz Prize for Poetry. He lives in St. Louis.

Robert B. Shaw is the author of several books of poetry, including *Solving for X*, *The Post Office Murals Restored*, and *Below the Surface*. He is professor of English at Mount Holyoke College and lives in Florence, Massachusetts.

Louis Simpson was born in Jamaica, West Indies. Among his more than twenty collections of poetry are *There You Are*; *In the Room We Share*; *Collected Poems*; *People Live Here: Selected Poems 1949–83*; *Searching for the Ox*; *Adventures of the Letter I*; *Selected Poems*; and *At the End of the Open Road, Poems*, winner of the Pulitzer Prize. His books of criticism include *Ships Going into the Blue: Essays and Notes on Poetry*, *The Character of the Poet*, *A Company of Poets*, and *A Revolution in Taste: Studies of Dylan Thomas, Allen Ginsberg, Sylvia Plath, and Robert Lowell*. He is also the author of a memoir, *The King My Father's Wreck*, and *Selected Prose*. He lives in Setauket, New York.

Floyd Skloot is the author of *Evening Light*, *The Fiddler's Trance*, and *Music Appreciation*, collections of poems; *In the Shadow of Memory* and *The Night-Side*, collections of essays; and *The Open Door*, *Summer Blue*, and *Pilgrim's Harbor*, novels. He lives in Amity, Oregon.

Dave Smith is the author of seventeen collections of poems, including *The Wick of Memory: New and Selected Poems 1970–2000* and *Fate's Kite: Poems, 1991–1995*. He also is the author of *Onliness*, a novel, and *Southern Delights*, a collection of short stories. *Local Assays: On Contemporary American Poetry* and *The Pure Clear Word: Essays on the Poetry of James Wright* are collections of his criticism. He is Boyd Professor of English and co-editor of the *Southern Review* at Louisiana State University. He lives in Baton Rouge, Louisiana.

George Jay Smith, writer and educator, was born in Lebanon, Ohio, in 1866. Author of many grammar books and reference books on literature, he is most remembered for his one-act play *Forbidden Fruit* (1915). He was a frequent contributor to such journals as the *Saturday Evening Post*, *Life*, *Argosy*, *Harper's Weekly*, and *North American Review*. Smith most likely heard Helen Keller speak at the May 31, 1918, meeting of the Walt Whitman Fellowship in New York, hosted by Horace Traubel. Smith died in 1937.

William Stafford published more than sixty books of poetry and prose, including *Traveling through the Dark*, winner of the National Book Award for Poetry in 1963. Stafford taught at Lewis and Clark College in Portland, Oregon, for more than thirty years. He died in 1993. His posthumous collection, *The Way It Is: New and Selected Poems*, was published in 1998.

Gerald Stern is the author of more than a dozen collections of poems, most recently *Amer-*

222

*ican Sonnets, Last Blue,* and *This Time: New and Selected Poems,* winner of the 1998 National Book Award for poetry. He lives in New Jersey, where he was appointed that state's first poet laureate.

Tim Suermondt is the author of *The Dangerous Women with Their Cellos* and *Greatest Hits,* both collections of poetry. He is an executive recruiter of stockbrokers and lives in Jamaica, New York.

Phil Tabakow's poems have appeared in numerous magazines and journals, including *Cincinnati Poetry Review, Colorado Review,* and *Denver Quarterly.* He twice held the Elliston Poetry Foundation poetry fellowship at the University of Cincinnati and teaches at Bridgewater State College in Massachusetts.

Richard Terrill is the author of *Fakebook: Improvisations on a Journey Back to Jazz* and *Saturday Night in Baoding,* both memoirs. His translations from Chinese and Korean have appeared in many journals. He teaches in the MFA Program in Creative Writing at Minnesota State University, Mankato.

Eric Torgersen is the author of *At War with Friends, The Door to the Moon,* and *Good True Stories,* collections of poems; *Ethiopia,* a novella; and *Dear Friend: Rainer Maria Rilke and Paula Modersohn-Becker,* a study of the relationship between the poet and the painter. He is professor of English at Central Michigan University and lives in Mount Pleasant, Michigan.

David Wagoner has published more than fifteen collections of poetry, among them *Traveling Light: Collected and New Poems; Walt Whitman Bathing; Through the Forest: New and Selected Poems; Who Shall Be the Sun? Poems Based on the Lore, Legends, and Myths of Northwest Coast and Plateau Indians;* and *Collected Poems, 1956–1976,* nominated for the National Book Award. He is also the author of ten novels. He has edited *Poetry Northwest* since 1966 and taught at the University of Washington. He lives in Bothell, Washington.

Diane Wakoski has published more than twenty collections of poetry. Her most recent is *The Butcher's Apron: New and Selected Poems.* Her essays have been collected in *Toward a New Poetry, Variations on a Theme, Creating a Personal Mythology,* and *Form Is an Extension of Content.* She has been writer-in-residence at Michigan State University since 1976.

Anne Waldman — author most recently of *Marriage: A Sentence* and *Vow to Poetry: Essays Interviews, Manifestos* — is Distinguished Professor of Poetics at the Jack Kerouac School of Disembodied Poetics at Naropa University, a creative writing program she co-founded with Allen Ginsberg in 1974. Her recent CD is *Alchemical Elegy* from the William Burroughs Virus Word Lab. She lives in Boulder, Colorado.

Theodore Weiss has published fourteen volumes of poetry, the latest being his *Selected Poems.* For over fifty years he and his wife Renée have edited the *Quarterly Review of Literature.* Recently they won a PEN Club Special Lifetime Award for their editing; and Weiss received the Oscar Williams and Gene Derwood Award for his poetry. They are completing a collaborative volume of poems. He is emeritus professor of literature at Princeton University in Princeton, New Jersey, where they live.

Gail White is the author of *The Price of Everything* and the editor of *Landscapes with Women: Four Poets*. She lives in Breaux Bridge, Louisiana.

Wang Yin was born in Shanghai in 1962 and graduated from Shanghai Teacher's University. He is widely published in journals throughout China. "Walt Whitman" was his first poem published in translation in America.

Jake Adam York's poems have appeared in such journals as *Greensboro Review*, *Poet Lore*, *Shenandoah*, *Southern Poetry Review*, the *Southern Review*, and the *Texas Review*. He serves as contributing editor to *Shenandoah Review*. He teaches American literature and creative writing at the University of Colorado at Denver.

# Permissions

We are grateful to the authors, editors, and publishers who have given us permission to reprint poems.

Sherman Alexie, "Defending Walt Whitman." Reprinted from *The Summer of Black Widows* © copyright 1996 by Sherman Alexie, by permission of Hanging Loose Press.

Eugénio de Andrade, "Walt Whitman and the Birds." From *Memory of Another River* (New Rivers Press, 1988). © 1988 by Alexis Levitin. Reprinted by permission of the translator, Alexis Levitin.

Aliki Barnstone, "Wild With It." From *Wild With It* (Sheep Meadow Press, 2002). © 2002 by Aliki Barnstone. Reprinted by permission of the publisher.

Tony Barnstone, "Hair of the Field." From *Impure* (University Press of Florida, 1999). © 1999 by Tony Barnstone. Reprinted by permission of the publisher.

Willis Barnstone, "Jiang Yuying, Famous Professor at Beijing University, Who Daringly Rendered into Chinese the First Complete Walt Whitman." From *5 A.M. in Beijing* (Sheep Meadow Press, 1987). © 1987 by Willis Barnstone. Reprinted by permission of the author.

Marvin Bell, "Whitman's Grass." From *Massachusetts Review* 33 (spring 1992). © 1992 by Marvin Bell. Reprinted by permission of the author.

Joe Benevento, "May 31, 1989," first appeared in *Galley Sail Review*, series 2, issue 36, spring 1990. © 1989 by Joe Benevento. Reprinted by permission of the author.

Ted Berrigan, "Whitman in Black." Excerpted from *So Going Around Cities: New & Selected Poems 1958–1979*. Copyright © 1980 by Ted Berrigan. Reprinted here by permission of Blue Wind Press.

John Berryman, "Despair." From *Collected Poems: 1937–1971 by John Berryman*. Copyright © 1989 by Kate Donahue Berryman. Reprinted by permission of Farrar, Straus and Giroux, LLC.

Robert Bly, "This Night: For Walt Whitman." © 2003 by Robert Bly. Reprinted by permission of the author.

Jorge Luis Borges, "Camden, 1892," first appeared in *Holiday Magazine*, November 1975. © 1975 by Willis Barnstone. Reprinted by permission of the translator, Willis Barnstone.

Michael Dennis Browne, "Your Sister." © 2003 by Michael Dennis Browne. Reprinted by permission of the author.

Joseph Bruchac, "Canticle." From *Flow* (Cold Mountain, 1972). © 1972 by Joseph Bruchac. Reprinted by permission of the author.

Edward Byrne, "Early Evening." From *East of Omaha* (Pecan Grove Press, 1998). © 1998 by Edward Byrne. Reprinted by permission of the author.

Thomas Centolella, "Small Acts." From *Terra Firma*. Copyright © 1990 by Thomas Centolella. Reprinted by permission of Copper Canyon Press.

Nicholas Christopher, "Walt Whitman at the Reburial of Poe," first appeared in *New Yorker*, August 25, 1980. © 1980 by Nicholas Christopher. Reprinted by permission of the author.

David Citino, "Walt Whitman in New Orleans, 1848." From *Last Rites and Other Poems* (Ohio State University Press, 1979). © 1979 by David Citino. Reprinted by permission of the author.

Jonathan Cohen, "Walt Whitman in Ohio," originally appeared in *Agni Review*, no. 24/25, 1987. © 1987 by Jonathan Cohen. Reprinted by permission of the author.

Gillian Conoley, "Walt Whitman in the Car Lot, Repo or Used," first appeared in *North American Review*, June 1989; reprinted in *Tall Stranger* (Carnegie Mellon University Press, 1991). © 1989 by Gillian Conoley. Reprinted by permission of the author.

David Cope, "Labor Day." From *Quiet Lives* (Humana Press, 1983). © 1983 by David Cope. Reprinted by permission of the author.

Bruce Cutler, "February 12, 1865." Excerpted from *The Massacre at Sand Creek: Narrative Voices* (University of Oklahoma Press, 1995). © 1995 by Bruce Cutler. Reprinted by permission of Emily Cutler.

Philip Dacey, "Whitman: The Wall." From *Sycamore Review*, summer 1995, and *What's Empty Weighs the Most: 24 Sonnets* (Black Dirt Press, 1997). © 1997 by Philip Dacey. Reprinted by permission of the author.

Toi Derricotte, "Whitman, Come Again to the Cities." From *Captivity* by Toi Derricotte. Copyright © 1989. Reprinted by permission of the University of Pittsburgh Press.

W. S. Di Piero, "Walt, the Wounded." From *The Dog Star* (University of Massachusetts Press, 1990). © 1990 by W. S. Di Piero. Reprinted by permission of the author.

Mark Doty, "Letter to Walt Whitman." From *Source* (HarperCollins, 2002). © 2001 by Mark Doty. Reprinted by permission of the author and the publisher.

Richard Eberhart, "Centennial for Whitman." From *Collected Poems 1930–1986* by Richard Eberhart. Copyright © 1960, 1976, 1987 by Richard Eberhart. Used by permission of Oxford University Press, Inc.

Lynn Emanuel, "Walt, I Salute You!" From *Then, Suddenly —* by Lynn Emanuel. Copyright © 1999. Reprinted by permission of the University of Pittsburgh Press.

Martín Espada, "Another Nameless Prostitute Says the Man Is Innocent." From *A Mayan*

*Astrologer in Hell's Kitchen* (Norton, 2000). © 2000 by Martín Espada. Reprinted by permission of the author.

Dave Etter, "Green-Eyed Boy after Reading Whitman and Sandburg." From *Selected Poems* (Spoon River Poetry Press, 1987). © 1987 by Dave Etter. Reprinted by permission of the author.

Richard Fein, "To Walt Whitman." From *Southern Review*, winter 2000. © 2000 by Richard J. Fein. Reprinted by permission of the author.

Lawrence Ferlinghetti, "Poem for Old Whitman." From *These Are My Rivers*. Copyright © 1993 by Lawrence Ferlinghetti. Reprinted by permission of New Directions Publishing Corp.

Calvin Forbes, "Reading Walt Whitman." From *Blue Monday* (Wesleyan University Press, 1974). © 1974 by Calvin Forbes. Reprinted by permission of the author.

Randall Freisinger, "Walt Whitman at Timber Creek," first appeared in *Mickle Street Review*, no. 7, 1985; subsequently published in *Running Patterns* (Flume Press, 1985). © 1985 by Randall Freisinger. Reprinted by permission of the author.

Daisy Fried, "A Story Having to Do with Walt Whitman," originally appeared in *The Threepenny Review*, winter 1999; subsequently published in *She Didn't Mean to Do It* (University of Pittsburgh Press, 2001). Copyright © 2001 by Daisy Fried. Reprinted by permission of the University of Pittsburgh Press.

Thomas Gannon, "Meeting the Master." © 2002 by Thomas Gannon. Reprinted by permission of the author.

Suzanne Gardinier, "Memorials," in "Book One" from *The New World*. Copyright © 1993 by Suzanne Gardinier. Reprinted by permission of the University of Pittsburgh Press.

Allen Ginsberg, "I Love Old Whitman So." From *White Shroud: Poems 1980–1985*. Copyright © 1986 by Allen Ginsberg. Reprinted by permission of HarperCollins Publishers Inc.

Jesse Glass, "Lecturing on Walt Whitman and Emily Dickinson in China." From *Literary Review* 39, summer 1996. © 1996 by Jesse Glass. Reprinted by permission of the author.

Patricia Goedicke, "For Walt Whitman." From *Crossing the Same River* (University of Massachusetts Press, 1985). © 1985 by Patricia Goedicke. Reprinted by permission of the author.

Albert Goldbarth, "The Poem of the Praises." From *Arts & Sciences* (Ontario Review Press, 1986). © 1986 by Albert Goldbarth. Reprinted by permission of the publisher.

Beckian Fritz Goldberg, "Whitman's Confession: In the Cleft of Eternity." From *Never Be the Horse* (University of Akron Press, 1999). © 1995 by Beckian Fritz Goldberg. Reprinted by permission of the author.

# Index to Titles